PHILIP AND THE
REVIVAL IN
SAMARIA

PHILIP AND THE REVIVAL IN SAMARIA

Geoffrey Thomas

THE BANNER OF TRUTH TRUST

THE BANNER OF TRUTH TRUST
3 Murrayfield Road, Edinburgh EH12 6EL, UK
P.O. Box 621, Carlisle, PA 17013, USA

*

© Geoffrey Thomas 2005
ISBN 0 85151 899 0

*

Typeset in 12 /15 pt Sabon at the
Banner of Truth Trust, Edinburgh
Printed in the U.S.A. by
Versa Press, Inc.,
East Peoria, IL.

CONTENTS

1

THE MAN GOD USED

Pick out from among you seven men of good repute, full of
the Spirit and of wisdom (*Acts* 6:3).

The story of the great awakening that took place in
Samaria is recounted for us in Acts chapter 8. The
person God used in that extraordinary display of his grace
was a man called Philip. We must not confuse this Philip
– often referred to as Philip the evangelist (*Acts* 21:8) –
with Philip the apostle, one of our Lord's twelve disciples
(*John* 1:43–48; *John* 6:5; *John* 12:21; *John* 14:8).

We know nothing of Philip's background; we do not
know in what kind of family he was raised or how he
became a Christian. He is introduced to us in connection
with the appointment of seven 'servers' or deacons by
the church in Jerusalem (*Acts* 6:1–7). This, it seems, is
how Philip began to serve his Lord. I wonder how many
preachers began working for the Lord by getting involved
in humble and unglamorous acts of service within their
home church? Perhaps their record of service began with
Sunday School teaching, or taking an active part in the
prayer meeting, or leading the young people's work,
or by being appointed to serve as a deacon within the
fellowship.

Serious tensions arose within the Jerusalem church as the number of converts increased. A particular pressure grew out of the church's daily distribution of food to poor members of the congregation. In those days there were no government welfare agencies to care for those in need. We can well imagine how attractive a group of people would seem to be who provided a daily meal for their elderly widows and human nature being what it is, there were always 'freeloaders' turning up and professing to be followers of Jesus Christ in order to get a free lunch. It would be no surprise if a coolness was shown to poor people arriving at the church building, while excitement would greet a rich person who attended church for the first time (*James* 2:2–3).

It was not long before there was within the early church a definite group of women known as 'true widows, left alone' (*1 Tim.* 5:3, 5). Paul also makes mention of a list of widows in his letter to Timothy; to be on this list a woman had to have been faithful to her husband, and well known for her good deeds (*1 Tim.* 5:9). Such widows were eligible for the daily provision of food. Individual Christians were expected to look after their own widowed family members, and not burden the church with them so that the church can help those widows who are really in need (*1 Tim.* 5:16). The amount of space Paul devotes in his first letter to Timothy shows us that a ministry of mercy was clearly an important part of the work and witness of the early Christian church.

Initially, the apostles supervised this daily distribution of food. Caring for the needy was a Christian obligation. The same Spirit-filled apostles who preached the word so boldly on the day of Pentecost are now engaged in the rather mundane task of waiting on tables and serving widows. In their thinking there was no conflict between Spirit-filled preaching and Spirit-filled caring.

Similarly, hundreds of years later there was no conflict in the heart of George Whitefield, the eighteenth-century evangelist of the Great Awakening in Britain and North America, between preaching the gospel to thousands almost every day of his life and the establishment of a home for orphans in Savannah, Georgia, in what was then England's poorest colony. His ministry of mercy to these poor boys was a burden that he gladly carried throughout his life. Throughout the ages Christians have been involved in ministering to the poor and needy members of society. Almshouses, hospitals, schools, and orphanages have characterised the church's ministry of mercy from earliest times. Such Christian men as Charles Spurgeon, Dr Barnardo, and George Muller who also built houses for orphans in the nineteenth century did not forget George Whitefield's example. Like the apostles, the priority of these men was the preaching of the gospel but they also cared for the hungry and needy.

As the work of the gospel grew and as the pressures of the work increased there was a danger that the care of the widows would absorb too much of the apostles' energy and endanger their primary responsibilities in connection with the ministry of the Word and prayer. It was the Twelve themselves who came to see this. They said, 'It is not right for us that we should give up preaching the word of God in order to serve tables' (*Acts* 6:2). What follows on from this apostolic statement is the emergence of the office of deacon within the Christian church. However important the physical well being of the needy is, the spiritual ministry of the gospel must take precedence and is therefore inviolable. The Lord directed the apostles to remain, above everything else, men of prayer and preachers of the gospel.

So it was in this diaconal ministry of mercy that Philip's work for the Lord began. The church selected him for his graciousness in ministering to elderly widows. This is how his life of fruitful Christian service began. He 'served tables' and addressed the tensions that existed between the Greek and Palestinian Jews within the Christian church at Jerusalem. One might think that Philip would have been better prepared for his great awakening ministry in some other way. Would he not have been better prepared for this great task by being trained by the apostles, and then putting his preaching skills to the test in small, sympathetic groups of believers within the fellowship of the church? But the fact is that he began his full-time Christian service by caring for the vulnerable, and sometimes quarrelsome, old women in the congregation. Perhaps, today, we put too much emphasis on the benefits of gaining experience in the work of preaching and not enough emphasis on the development of Christian character through the loving and patient service of others.

Philip must have learned many valuable lessons while helping these frail elderly people. He would have been careful not to patronise or demean them, but rather to consider each one better than himself, encouraging them to be proud of their high position in Christ, showing them love in the name of the Lord Jesus, and believing that in doing something for the least of Christ's disciples, he was doing it for his Lord. Philip was 'full of the Spirit' and this made him like his Lord. At that very moment when the awful, dark shadow of Calvary fell upon Jesus, he set his disciples an astonishing example of humble service. Like a model household slave, Jesus took the towel and basin of water, knelt down before each of his disciples, and washed their feet. 'When he had washed their feet and put on his outer garments and resumed his place, he said to them, "Do you understand what I have done to you? You call me Teacher and Lord, and you are right, for so I am. If I then, your Lord and Teacher, have washed your feet, you also ought to wash one another's feet. For I have given you an example, that you also should do just as I have done to you. Truly, truly, I say to you, a servant is not greater than his master, nor is a messenger greater than the one who sent him. If you know these things, blessed are you if you do them' (*John* 13:12–17).

The Scriptures teach us that God opposes the proud but gives grace to the humble (*1 Pet.* 5:5). God gave his grace to humble Philip. It is not beyond the realms of possibility that there could have been an awakening in Samaria if Philip had not humbly performed the task to which the Jerusalem church appointed him. But the fact remains that the man God chose to use to bring the gospel to Samaria – and with such tremendous power – had this particular background and character. Jesus taught his disciples to think humbly about themselves and their service in the kingdom of God: 'Let the greatest among you become as the youngest, and the leader as one who serves' (*Luke* 22:26). Thus it was with Philip, a humble servant of the Lord. He did not quibble with the church's appointment saying, 'God has not called me to wait on tables; he has called me to be a preacher!' No, he humbly accepted the responsibility conferred on him and counted it an honour to serve Christ and his people in this way, little knowing that faithfully serving the needy was to be an essential part of his preparation for what was probably the greatest task of his life.

George Whitefield began his Christian life at a time when he was a servant in the kitchen and dining rooms of an Oxford college, waiting on his fellow students. Acting as a servitor was the only way he could pay for his university education. It was in this capacity that he met the Wesley brothers and became a member of the 'Holy Club'. Together with the other members of that club he made visits to Oxford jail and brought help and relief to the poor prisoners who were languishing there. In this way the remarkable and fruitful service of a great man of God began: being faithful in small things led to faithfulness in larger things.

Or consider the Scottish pastor Thomas Boston: at home in the manse he tenderly cared for his mentally ill wife; at church in the pulpit he preached the gospel with great power. If he had despised his domestic responsibilities could he have been such a channel of God's grace to his congregation? The discipline of life in the manse was part of the way God prepared him to preach a gospel that teaches submission to God and service of others. The pioneer missionary William Carey in India carried a similar burden. His first wife was afflicted with mental illness, and yet Carey ministered lovingly to her while at the same time he laboured faithfully to bring the good news of the gospel to the people of India. These men were tender-hearted servants like Philip whom God greatly used.

We must not come under the impression that Philip deliberately took on this vocation temporarily with an eye to his future preaching ministry. That would be a wrong conclusion to draw from this passage. Rather, Philip, it seems, readily answered the call of the church to this diaconal work – 'the whole gathering . . . chose . . . Philip' (*Acts* 6:5) – and he would have gladly spent the whole of his life doing just that, if the Lord had so willed it. Although the church called him to his diaconal task, there is no comparable call from the church by which Philip was set apart to preach the gospel in Samaria. In fact, it was the outbreak of persecution that led him to Samaria. Following the death of Stephen, 'there arose . . . a great persecution against the church in Jerusalem, and they were all scattered throughout the regions of Judea and Samaria, except the apostles . . . Philip went down to the city in Samaria and proclaimed to them the Christ' (Acts 8:1, 5). Everyone in the early church knew of their obligation to obey the Saviour's Great Commission to go into all the world and preach the gospel. 'Those who were scattered went about preaching the word' (*Acts* 8:4), and Philip took the word of Christ with him to the Samaritans.

The call to 'the Seven' to serve the needy together with the absence of a reference to Philip's ordination to preach the gospel, seems to indicate a pattern that does not correspond to the way we like to operate within the church. We tell our congregations, 'Let everyone get involved in caring for the poor,' while hoping against hope for enthusiastic volunteers to arise and come forward. Some poor, unfortunate deacon is put in charge of the rota for the care of the poor and he has to ensure that the irksome duties of serving are fulfilled by somebody – almost anybody – every day. The cry goes up, 'We need someone to serve tables this week. Will someone be kind enough to volunteer their services? The unglamorous task of caring for the poor can be left to volunteers, but let no one start evangelising unless there is a long meeting of the elders, and a lengthy discussion in a church meeting which may kill the whole project off by a thousand quali- fications, before permission is given! We like to regulate everything – except what we have judged to be the mun- dane and unglamorous Christian work, for which we cry out for volunteers. Yet it was in the serving of tables that Philip was prepared for his life's great work. Perhaps we need to change our priorities and declare with our Master that 'the greatest among you shall be your serv- ant' (*Matt.* 23:11).

When the church chose Philip for this service he had no idea that in a short space of time he would be leaving Jerusalem to preach to thousands of people in Samaria. He was content to do anything for Christ. God tested Philip by examining his willingness to work in this prac- tical task given him by the church. Philip was found faithful and, before long, the Lord moved him to another field of service. Philip and Stephen began their work for Christ through practical works of service, before the Lord moved them on to proclaim the gospel. It was impossible that two such powerful and original men could be re- stricted to serving tables. Perhaps Paul was thinking of them when he wrote to Timothy, 'Those who serve well as deacons gain a good standing for themselves and also great confidence in the faith that is in Christ Jesus' (*1 Tim.* 3:13).

Did this concern within the early church for feeding hungry old believers dampen the fires of the Spirit of God? Not at all! In fact the reverse was the case. The Seven are set aside for their work, and we are told in the next verse, 'And the word of God continued to increase, and the number of disciples multiplied greatly in Jerusalem, and a great many of the priests became obedient to the faith' (*Acts* 6:7). The same kind of thing has happened throughout the history of the church. People in nineteenth-century Bristol came to George Muller's assembly when they saw the fine orphan-houses he had erected on the Downs to look after his waifs and strays. In Taiwan the majority of the people, the Minna Chinese, were being restricted, harassed, and discriminated against by the minority Mandarin government. Christians spoke up about this injustice and helped the Minna Chinese, with the result that these burdened people became less critical of Christian activity and open to considering the message of the Christian missionaries.

PHILIP WAS FULL OF THE SPIRIT

We now need to consider, what was it that equipped Philip to help these poor widows? The rather surprising answer Luke supplies us with is the Holy Spirit of God. The apostles said to the church, 'Therefore, brothers, pick out from among you seven men of good repute, full of the Spirit and of wisdom' (*Acts* 6:3). There was no other way of glorifying God in this daily duty of feeding the poor in the name of Jesus Christ without the men responsible for it being full of the Spirit of God. In the absence of the Spirit food can be served on a table and the diners hurried away once it has been eaten, with everything done in a peremptory way. But these men had to be qualified for this task by being 'full of the Holy Spirit'.

Being full of the Holy Spirit is a well-known phrase, and has engendered some heated debates in Christian circles. One of the reasons for this controversy comes from the fact that the phrase 'being filled with the Spirit' is used in a number of different ways in the New Testament. We shall see that Scripture uses it in three main ways, and that this threefold fullness of the Spirit was evidenced in the life of Philip himself.

Firstly, Philip (like every believer in Jesus Christ) possessed the Holy Spirit at the centre of his being and in every facet of his life from the time he was born again of the Spirit. Secondly, as he became a more mature Christian Philip was full of the Holy Spirit in the sense that he was a godly and Christlike man. Thirdly, Philip was full of the Holy Spirit when God sovereignly enabled him to carry out a special work.

1. Full of the Spirit at Conversion: United to Christ

Let us consider how every Christian possesses the Holy Spirit at the centre of his being and in every facet of his life. This is a non-negotiable truth upon which every Christian ought to be agreed. Paul tells the Romans 'Anyone who does not have the Spirit of Christ does not belong to him' (*Rom.* 8:9). The Christian life begins by a 'conception' from above – we are 'born from above', 'born again', 'born of God', which enables us to take that first faltering step across the threshold of the kingdom of God (*John* 3:5). It is God himself who begins the saving work in sinners by his Spirit (*Phil.* 1:6). The Holy Spirit is also God's great gift to all who receive Christ. Peter, on the day of Pentecost, told the enquirers convicted by his sermon, 'Repent, and be baptized every one of you in the name of Jesus Christ for the forgiveness of your sins, and you will receive the gift of the Holy Spirit. For the promise is for you and for your children and for all who are far off, everyone whom the Lord our God calls to himself' (*Acts* 2:38–39). 'Here is a divine gift', says the apostle, 'and it is being offered to you right now. The gift is the Giver – God himself. Through his servants he is sincerely offering himself to you. Turn from your sins, believe in Christ, be baptized, and you will discover that this gift of God the Holy Spirit has already become yours.'

Paul tells the Roman church of 'the Holy Spirit who has been given to us' (*Rom.* 5:5), and the Thessalonian church of 'God, who gives his Holy Spirit to you' (*1 Thess.* 4:8). To the Corinthians he writes, 'Do you not know that your body is a temple of the Holy Spirit within you, whom you have from God?' (*1 Cor.* 6:19). Paul also informs them, 'He who has prepared us for this very thing is God, who has given us the Spirit as a guarantee' (*2 Cor.* 5:5). The apostle John also bears testimony to the indwelling presence of the Spirit as a gift from God: 'By this we know that he abides in us, by the Spirit whom he has given us' (*1 John* 3:24). Again he says, 'By this we know that we abide in him and he in us, because he has given us of his Spirit' (*1 John* 4:13). This marvellous gift of God's Spirit is offered freely to all who believe the gospel of Jesus Christ. From the moment of the first stirrings of new life in Christ within the heart of the believer this gift of God makes its presence known by creating distaste for sin and drawing the soul to trust and obey the Lord Jesus. All our new convictions and attitudes are the result of this free gift. God the Holy Spirit enters every believer's life. It is this reality that every Christian shares. There is no way that we can take the first step in following Christ without the presence and life-giving power of the Holy Spirit.

We cannot emphasize enough that everything is made new in the life of the person whom the Holy Spirit enters at the new birth. Every Christian is given a new heart (*Ezek.* 36:26) and a new spirit (*1 Pet.* 3:4). Every Christian finds rest in Christ (*Matt.* 11:29), their bodies are made the temple of the Holy Spirit (*1 Cor.* 6:19) and their minds are now set on things above (*Col.* 3:2). All this is true of the weakest lamb in the flock of Christ. The 'new kid on the Christian block' has all these privileges. There is not one believer in the whole world for whom these things, which God the Holy Spirit graciously works in them, are imaginary or fanciful or an exaggeration. 'I came that they may have life, and have it abundantly' is the word of Jesus' promise to every one of his people (*John* 10:10).

> 'Tis Thine to cleanse the heart,
> To sanctify the soul,
> To pour fresh life in every part,
> And new create the whole.
> *Joseph Hart*

However, not every Christian may understand the scope of the changes brought about in his life by the new birth. Some believers do not realize their magnificent status as children of God who are indwelt by the Holy Spirit (*1 Cor.* 6:15,19). Yet this is the amazing thing about all

Christians, even the one who is least in the kingdom of God. The Holy Spirit pervades the whole of his life, and there is no part of his life that is off-limits for the Spirit. That is the portion and lot of every believer, even for those who may not yet appreciate, as they should, just what the Lord has done for them in Christ and in them by his Spirit.

One implication of this great truth is that the Christian cannot blame the Lord for failing to do the will of God in his life. Not one believer may successfully argue that 'My resources were inadequate. The divine provision let me down.' For God will say, 'Did I not give you the Holy Spirit? Did you not have free access to his grace and power?' There is no part of our lives that has been neglected or ignored by God. 'Therefore, if anyone is in Christ, he is a new creation. The old has passed away; behold, the new has come' (2 *Cor.* 5:17). Whether in caring for the senile widow or the handicapped child, handling a broken heart, walking through the valley of the shadow of death, speaking a word for the Lord Jesus, resisting temptation, enduring affliction, or completing one's duties, every Christian can say, 'I can do all things through him who strengthens me' (*Phil.* 4:13).

So the Spirit indwells us, and his presence permeates every aspect of our existence, because God has poured out his Spirit upon every believer in the washing of regeneration. When you hear, therefore, of a Christian behaving abominably you must not say, 'Ah, the Spirit let him down.' Rather, you must say that he grieves the Spirit by his actions, and that he has taken the very Spirit of God with him into that compromising circumstance, and so on. We are all personally responsible and accountable for our actions. Though becoming holy is not within our natural grasp, we are nevertheless answerable for our sanctification. That is why the Scriptures command us to 'be holy' and to 'grow in the grace of the Lord Jesus Christ' (*1 Pet.* 1:15; *2 Pet.* 3:18). You cannot say that you would not have sinned in the way you did if only you had more of the Spirit. Think of Peter refusing to eat a meal with Gentile Christians in the church because they did not belong to the Jewish race. By every reckoning Peter was full of the Holy Spirit, and yet in this situation we are told that he acted hypocritically, not walking uprightly according to the truth of the gospel; 'He was to be blamed' (*Gal.* 2:11–12, AV).

2. *Full of the Spirit: Mature Christlike Character*

The mature Christian is a person who not only possesses the Holy Spirit by virtue of his union with Christ but is also full of the Holy Spirit in terms of his experience. It is surely in this sense that Luke is using this phrase in our text. The apostles could have said, 'Tap on the shoulder the first seven Christian men that leave the church and make them responsible for the widows' daily distribution because we know that every one of them possesses the Holy Spirit.' The apostles clearly instructed the church to look for a category of Christian men who were in some sense outstanding from the rest of the church members. In this instance the church was to look for men who were not novices (not newly born Christians), nor men who were backsliders and living in defiance of the will of God. It is tragically possible that we may find true Christians who are in a backslidden condition – 'neither cold nor hot' (*Rev.* 3:15), and others who have left their

first love (*Rev.* 2:4). You would not lightly say of such
people that they were 'full of the Holy Spirit', though
they are indwelt by him, and their bodies are the temple
of the Holy Spirit (*1 Cor.* 6:19).

So the phrase 'full of the Spirit' is used to describe
mature Christians. Consider Barnabas who is described
as 'a good man, full of the Holy Spirit and of faith' (*Acts*
11:24). We could equally well describe him by one of the
various New Testament terms that designate a mature
Christian. For example, he was clothed in the whole
armour of God; he had taken up his cross and denied
himself to follow Christ; he had presented his body as a
living sacrifice to God; he was living his life worthy of
the calling he had received; he was walking in the light;
he was an imitator of God; he was strong in the Lord and
in the power of his might; his attitude was the same as
that of Christ Jesus; he was standing firm in the Lord. In
such ways the New Testament portrays consistent Christian maturity. 'Full of the Holy Spirit' is just one way to
describe this Christian characteristic.

To understand what it meant for Philip to be full of the
Holy Spirit, we could do no better than turn to those
verses in the Pastoral Epistles that amplify the character-
istics expected of deacons. According to the apostle Paul,
Spirit-filled men are, 'dignified, not double-tongued, not
addicted to much wine, not greedy for dishonest gain.
They must hold the mystery of the faith with a clear conscience . . . the husband of one wife, managing their
children and households well' (*1 Tim.* 3:8–12). Or again
when Paul describes the elders in the same chapter, he
uses similar moral and spiritual terms: 'Therefore an over-
seer must be above reproach, the husband of one wife,

sober-minded, self-controlled, respectable, hospitable, able to teach, not a drunkard, not violent but gentle, not quarrelsome, not a lover of money . . . He must not be a recent convert, or he may become puffed up with conceit and fall into the condemnation of the devil. Moreover, he must be well thought of by outsiders, so that he may not fall into disgrace' (*1 Tim.* 3:2–7). Such a man is full of the Holy Spirit. Likewise, such a man has presented his body to Jesus Christ as a living sacrifice, is clothed in the whole armour of God, is growing in the grace of the Lord Jesus Christ, and so on. A mature Christian is full of the Spirit in the sense that he is controlled by the energies of the life-transforming and sanctifying Spirit. He is a humble man who knows that any good he has ever achieved in his life has been achieved only through the indwelling Spirit's work (*Phil.* 2:12–13).

It is this aspect of the Spirit's work which Paul refers to when he says, 'Be filled with the Spirit' (*Eph.* 5:18). He could have equally said, 'Put on the new self, created in the likeness of God in true righteousness and holiness' or 'live a life worthy of the calling you have received' or 'put on the full armour of God'. In fact he does say all those things as well in the same letter. They are all pleas for Christian maturity, and did you notice how they are all in the present tense? Paul is calling for present continuous action on the part of his readers. The Christian is to be continuously engaged in this task at all times – 'Go on offering your bodies to God as instruments of righteousness; go on putting on the Christian armour; go on living a worthy life; go on being filled with the Holy Spirit.' There ought not to be two categories of Christians such as the armour-wearing and the non-armour-wearing

Christians, the living-sacrifice and the non-living-sacrifice Christians, the Spirit-filled and non-Spirit filled Christians. Rather, by the nature of the case, there will be different degrees of growth, development, and sanctification, as Christians are daily changed from one degree of glory to another (2 *Cor.* 3:18).

Of course, there has never been a Christian who can point to an unblemished track record of perfect progress in sanctification. Every Christian is daily engaged in an unrelenting war against the world, the flesh, and the devil; sometimes battles against remaining sin are lost in the course of this war. No man, except our sinless Saviour, has ever been completely full of the Holy Spirit in the sense of a godlike character.

> And none, O Lord, have perfect rest,
>   For none are wholly free from sin;
> And they who fain would serve Thee best,
>   Are conscious most of wrong within.
>
>   *Henry Twells*

But every Christian longs to reach that sinless state, and knows he will attain it on the day when Jesus Christ returns. On the glorious day of resurrection the Spirit of God will be in us as he was in Jesus – without measure – and we will be full of Christ's glory. Then at last we shall be like him for we shall see Jesus (*1 John* 3:2). Until then, the mature Christian will take up his cross daily, clothe himself with the whole armour of God, present his body to God as a living sacrifice, strive to live a life worthy of his high calling, and be filled with the Holy Spirit (*1 John* 3:3).

By what means are these things to be done? By entering into the presence of God, or, more simply, by putting ourselves where God is. And where is God to be found? 'Where two or three are gathered in my name, there am I among them' (*Matt.* 18:20). The Lord is found in the midst of his people in the church. God is also to be found when we kneel down in private prayer. Jesus expected his disciples to worship his Father in the privacy of their own rooms and held out a wonderful promise when they did so: 'But when you pray, go into your room and shut the door and pray to your Father who is in secret. And your Father who sees in secret will reward you' (*Matt.* 6:6).

What Paul prayed for others we can pray for ourselves in such moments of private communion with God: 'Now may the God of peace himself sanctify you completely, and may your whole spirit and soul and body be kept blameless at the coming of our Lord Jesus Christ. He who calls you is faithful; he will surely do it' (*1 Thess.* 5:23, 24). Though we can never attain spiritual perfection here, yet we can make progress towards it, and we are encouraged to know that full sanctification is the certain goal for all of the children whom God has 'predestined to be conformed to the image of his Son' (*Rom.* 8:29).

The mature Christian, then, is full of the Holy Spirit. Philip and his six Christian brothers were appointed to this office in the early church on this basis. Their character, relationships, ambitions, and reactions were under the control of the Spirit, and the congregation saw that in their lives. They were perfectly suited for undertaking this demanding ministry of mercy within the congregation.

3. *Full of the Spirit: Special Divine Enabling for Particular Tasks*

The Bible also uses this phrase, 'being filled with the Spirit', to describe experiences of the power of God for a particular task. In the Old Testament we find many references to the Spirit coming upon men. For example, 'But the Spirit of the LORD clothed Gideon' (*Judg.* 6:34). Or again we read that Samuel says to Saul, 'The Spirit of the LORD will rush upon you, and you will prophesy' (*1 Sam.* 10:6). Indeed, that is exactly what happened to Saul, 'When they came to Gibeah, behold, a group of prophets met him, and the Spirit of God rushed upon him, and he prophesied among them' (*1 Sam.* 10:10). Likewise, when the son of Jesse was anointed by Samuel in the presence of his brothers, 'the Spirit of the LORD rushed upon David from that day forward' (*1 Sam.* 16:13).

It is important for us to note that none of these men went through a number of 'steps' before the Spirit of God came upon them in this fashion. It is not even the case that they had reached a certain height of spirituality, having shaken off their coldness of heart, indifference, and lethargy. What we read of here is something entirely different. The Hebrew word used to describe the coming of the Spirit on these men is the same word used for a man putting on a jacket. Writing about the Reformation as a sovereign act of God, Professor Benne Holwerda of the Netherlands referred to this Old Testament image of a man putting on a coat:

> Now, we all know that when it's time to get to work, we
> put on our work clothes. The doctor has his white smock,

the labourer has his overalls, and the maid her apron. Yet
no one is so foolish as to ascribe the work he is about to
do to his work clothes. The act of putting on work clothes
does not signify that one's uniform is about to get to work;
rather, it indicates the moment at which the workman
himself, wearing those clothes, begins work. The patient
does not look to a white coat to heal him; yet when he
sees the doctor putting on that white coat, he knows that
he means to get to work.

Well, what we actually read here is that the Spirit of
the Lord puts Gideon on; that is to say, Gideon is to the
Spirit what overalls are to the worker. Gideon is only a
set of work clothes – the one doing the work is the Spirit.
And so we see that it is not Gideon who springs into action, but the Spirit. The Lord arises to do battle. What we
get here, then, is not the story of the great deeds of a
certain person but a report about the mighty deeds of the
Lord.[1]

Sinclair Ferguson confirms this interpretation: 'When
the Spirit "comes" on an individual, he "clothes himself" with that person's life, conforming it to his own
purposes.'[2] A person becomes 'another man' when the
Spirit takes him and clothes himself with him. The mental faculties are augmented, while the powers of expression
and the capacity to feel the truth of God are enlarged
beyond the ordinary measure of nature. There is no way
that the man's subsequent life can be explained in terms
of heredity, upbringing, and intelligence alone. The Spirit
has clothed himself with that person.

[1] Rudolf van Reest, *Schilder's Struggle for the Unity of the Church*
(Neerlandia: Inheritance Publications, 1990) p. 114.
[2] Sinclair B. Ferguson, *The Holy Spirit* (Leicester: IVP, 1996) p. 38.

In the first chapter of Luke's Gospel we are told about
two Old Testament believers, Elizabeth and Zechariah,
the parents of John the Baptist: 'And Elizabeth was filled
with the Holy Spirit, and she exclaimed with a loud cry,
Blessed are you among women . . .' (*Luke* 1:41–42).
Again, 'Zechariah was filled with the Holy Spirit and
prophesied' (*Luke* 1:67). The only explanation for their
actions and words is that the Holy Spirit came upon them
in this special way. They prophesied because God came
upon them by his Spirit and enabled them to prophesy.
The Spirit 'clothed himself' or 'put on' Gideon; the Spirit
'filled' Elizabeth and Zechariah. The subsequent effects
were remarkable.

Thus, the Spirit of God can come suddenly upon a
divinely chosen instrument. That person will be 'filled
with the Holy Spirit' for a special work – such as pro-
phetically speaking the words of God, or declaring the
Word of God with clarity, power, and convicting force.

On the day of Pentecost, the disciples in Jerusalem were
all 'filled with the Holy Spirit' and one of the miraculous
consequences of that Spirit-filling was that they 'began to
speak in other tongues, as the Spirit gave them utterance'
(*Acts* 2:4). This miracle signified that the exalted Christ
temporarily lifted aspects of the curse of Babel. The
nations, formerly divided by their languages, were able to
understand the greatest news on earth. Then Peter preached
in the power of the Spirit and his words awakened the
people of Jerusalem (*Acts* 2:4, 37). His preaching was de-
livered with the authority of heaven. The sword of the
Spirit was thrust into Jerusalem's sinners – 'they were cut
to the heart' and cried out, 'What shall we do?' Peter told
them to repent, and, astonishingly, three thousand people

received his message, and were baptized and added to their number on 'that day'.

What a day that was when the Spirit of God clothed himself with Peter! We cannot but wonder if Philip the evangelist was amongst the three thousand converted at Pentecost. Whether he was or was not, there can be no doubt that he knew what had taken place on that wonderful occasion. Pentecost established a benchmark in the understanding of the church as to what constitutes true preaching. The gospel of Christ must be preached to sinners 'by the Holy Spirit sent from heaven' (1 Pet. 1:12). Philip's convictions were surely shaped by the never-to-be-forgotten experience of the church on the day of Pentecost.

Here then is the prototype of a great religious awakening; Pentecost is the inaugural revival of the era known as 'the last days'. Sinclair Ferguson defines revival as 'the unstopping of the pent-up energies of the Spirit of God breaking down the dams which have been erected against his convicting and converting ministry in whole communities of individuals, as happened at Pentecost and in the "awakenings" which have followed.'[3]

Peter's preaching was of a man 'filled with the Spirit'. History records the powerful effects of the preaching ministries of other men down through the ages that were characterized by great power and unusual success. C. H. Spurgeon was filled with the Spirit, not for the special task of being the Lord's apostle or prophet (such offices belonged to the period in which Christ laid the foundation for his church), but to be a remarkably effective evangelist and pastor. Through him many souls were saved and a

[3] Ibid, p. 90.

large, strong, and fruitful local church was edified. His preaching was full of God, as though 'God [was] making his appeal through [him]' (2 *Cor.* 5:20). The same Spirit who inspired the human authors of Scripture may still come upon preachers and their congregations today. During such wonderful 'visitations' many are regenerated and God's people are reinvigorated in every Christian grace.

In a 'revived' church the preacher's words possess a special empowering as the Spirit uses them to bear witness to Jesus Christ. Jonathan Edwards, the 'theologian of revival' is often quoted, and his words bear repeating:

> It may be observed that from the Fall of man to this day wherein we live, the work of redemption in its effect has mainly been carried on by remarkable pourings out of the Spirit of God. Though there is a more constant influence of God's Spirit always in some degree attending His ordinances, yet the way in which the greatest things have been done towards carrying on the work always has been by remarkable pourings out of the Spirit at special seasons of mercy.[4]

The apostle Peter speaks of these 'special seasons of mercy' in this way: 'Repent therefore, and turn again, that your sins may be blotted out, that times of refreshing may came from the Lord, and that he may send the Christ appointed for you' (*Acts* 3:19–20). Peter speaks about the removal of sin, the sovereign refreshings, and of Christ being sent to those who repent and turn again. This suggests that the Spirit comes more than once only. Times of spiritual awakening, refreshing, and revival are due to his special visitations.

---

[4] Jonathan Edwards, *A History of the Work of Redemption* (1774; repr. Edinburgh: Banner of Truth, 2003) p. 35.

Such an awakening occurred in Scotland during the late sixteenth century when Robert Bruce was preaching in St Giles' Cathedral, Edinburgh. Robert Fleming described Bruce's ministry in these terms:

> Whilst Robert Bruce was in the ministry at Edinburgh he shined as a great light through the whole land, the power and efficacy of the Spirit most sensibly accompanying the word he preached . . . Bruce's speech and his preaching was in such evidence and demonstration of the Spirit that by the shining of his face, and that shower of divine influence, wherewith the word spoken was accompanied, it was easy for the hearer to perceive that he had been on the mount with God . . . he preached ordinarily with such life and power, and the word spoken by him was accompanied with such a manifest presence, that it was evident to the hearers that he was not alone at the work . . . some of the most-stout-hearted of his hearers were ordinarily made to tremble, and by having these doors which formerly had been bolted against Jesus Christ, as by an irresistible power broke open, and the secrets of their hearts made manifest, they went away under convictions and carrying with them undeniable proofs of Christ speaking in him.[5]

The American theologian, Charles Hodge, who had also known something of true awakenings in his lifetime, preached a sermon on 'The Revival of Religion'. In it he made an interesting remark about whether revivals were *the best way* for the church to advance.

---

[5] Robert Fleming, *The Fulfilling of the Scripture*, vol. 1, pp. 365, 378.

They are great mercies, but there are greater. When there have been years of famine a superabundant harvest is a great blessing. But it had been better had each harvest been good. There is a better state as well as a greater amount of good in the latter case than in the former case. A regular normal increase is better than violent alterations. General permanent health is better than exuberant joyousness alternating with depression.[6]

I once quoted those words to Dr Martyn Lloyd-Jones during a day conference on revival. He replied, 'Of course that is true, but *we* have had many years without a good harvest. We have *no* alternative.'

So Christ baptized his church with the Holy Spirit on the Day of Pentecost, as John the Baptist had prophesied, and the disciples were all filled with the Spirit. There was a monumental numerical advance in the kingdom of God from Christ's 'little flock' to several thousands. A 'new nation' was born in a day. The word was heard in Zion and soon went out into all the earth. Pentecost was the epicentre of an evangelical earthquake that continued to give further after-shocks. Following a time of prayer a few weeks later, these same Christians, 'were all filled with the Holy Spirit and continued to speak the word of God with boldness' (*Acts* 4:29–31). In other words, there were further occasions in the lives of these people when the Holy Spirit used them in this extraordinarily powerful and fruitful manner. God's almighty Spirit clothed himself with them time and again, and as a result they were enabled to act in a manner that could not be explained in natural terms. They had an extraordinary

[6] Charles Hodge, *Princeton Sermons* (Edinburgh: Banner of Truth, 1979) p. 340.

power given to them for such tasks as ruling, triumphing in battle, prophesying, preaching, speaking in other languages, and illuminating the church.

I once asked Professor John Murray about such experiences of the Holy Spirit, and he told me of something that happened during his own ministry. At a critical time in his denomination's history he was asked to clarify an issue that had arisen and which had potentially damaging consequences. As he prepared himself to address the issue he was very conscious of the gravity of the situation facing him. When he finally presented his convictions to the General Assembly he was extremely thankful that a spirit of understanding and harmony was given to the members of the church. The matter was resolved peacefully; the brothers were united and went forward together. What might have been a cause of schism instead became a means of strengthening the ties of fellowship.

We must always remember that the filling of the Spirit is never for the sake of the experience itself. The New Testament Christians at Pentecost were filled with the Spirit for a purpose: 'You will receive power when the Holy Spirit has come upon you, and you will be my witnesses' (*Acts* 1:8). I wonder whether there is not some reference to this purpose in the fact that, on almost every occasion when a Christian is described as being full of the Spirit, there is a 'plus'. For example, we are told that the seven 'deacons' were 'full of the Spirit and wisdom' (*Acts* 6:3). In other words, this ministry to the two groups of widows was a sensitive area that required great wisdom. The Grecian Jews were complaining that the Palestinian widows were being shown favouritism in the daily distribution. It was a delicate situation that could

have destroyed the life and witness of the church in its
infancy. Men of wisdom were needed to manage this delicate matter – that is, men full of the Spirit who would act
wisely within the church. The deacon's Spirit-fullness
would be shown through his wisdom in serving the
church.

Stephen is spoken of as a man who was 'full of the
Spirit and of wisdom' (*Acts* 6:3), 'full of faith and of the
Holy Spirit' (*Acts* 6:5), and 'full of God's grace and power'
(*Acts* 6:8). He was soon to face fierce opposition to his
ministry from the 'Synagogue of the Freedmen'. These
men rose up and disputed with Stephen. 'But they could
not withstand the wisdom and Spirit with which he was
speaking' (*Acts* 6:9–10). His fullness of God's power was
seen in his ability to courageously withstand all their at-
tacks upon the gospel he was preaching.

Think also of the description of Barnabas, 'He was a
good man, full of the Holy Spirit and of faith' (*Acts* 11:24).
His ministry was one in which he 'exhorted them all to
remain faithful to the Lord with steadfast purpose' (*Acts*
11:23). He displayed the grace of faith in his own life,
because he, himself, completely trusted in his God, what-
ever the consequences. Barnabas was 'full of faith'. The
description of the Christians in Iconium is also very
revealing: 'And the disciples were filled with joy and with
the Holy Spirit' (*Acts* 13:52). There was an outburst of
persecution against Paul and Barnabas and they were
expelled from the adjoining region. It would have been
easy for the believers to become bitter or self-pitying or
retaliatory, but they were given grace to rejoice even in
the midst of their hardships. They were filled with the
Holy Spirit and joy.

The experience of being filled with the Holy Spirit, especially in the great initiatory bestowal of the Spirit, is also described as being 'baptized in the Spirit'. The terms 'baptized with the Spirit' and 'filled with the Spirit' are closely linked in the Pentecost narrative. 'Baptism' refers to the initial definitive work; being 'filled with the Spirit' refers to the pervasive consequences of the Spirit's presence and activity in the life of the believer, sanctifying and at times empowering the believer for special works of service.

Now, every single Christian as far as their state is concerned is *filled* with the Holy Spirit in the sense that they have been baptized with the Holy Spirit: 'For in one Spirit we were *all* baptized into one body . . . and *all* were made to drink of one Spirit' (*1 Cor.* 12:13). But there are also these special occasions when a judge, or a king, or a priest, or a prophet, or an apostle, or the whole church is filled with the Holy Spirit *in a different sense*. The Lord sends the Spirit upon believers like Philip, Stephen, Peter, Paul and fills them for a special calling or work. This is like the Lord giving to his church a Luther, or a Whitefield, or a Spurgeon. There is no way we can predict that this year or next we are going to see the heavens opened and the Spirit of God poured out upon an individual or a church. Such outpourings and fillings of the Spirit are God's grand prerogative to give and in that honour none shall share. It is enough for us to know that they occur, and that we may inquire of the Lord for them. 'It is time for the LORD to act, for your law has been broken' (*Psa.* 119:126).

Consider what happened to the apostle Paul at Paphos. He was speaking of the Lord Jesus to Sergius Paulus the proconsul, when Elymas, a sorcerer, tried to dissuade him from being won over by Paul's words. We are told, 'But Saul, who was also called Paul, filled with the Holy Spirit, looked intently at him and said, "You son of the devil, you enemy of all righteousness . . ."' (*Acts* 13:9–10). The rebuke that came from a man who was baptized with the Spirit was solemn and utterly devastating for Elymas, and the result was that the proconsul, witnessing all this, believed 'for he was astonished at the teaching of the Lord' (*Acts* 13:12).

Think also of Martin Luther on trial at the Diet of Worms for his writings and especially his teaching concerning justification by faith alone. At the beginning of the Council Luther was shy, nervous, humble, and very much alone. But during the night (which he spent working on his statement), he was transformed. Dr James Atkinson says, 'The next day at four he appeared again. But it was a different Luther: utterly restored, completely self-composed and reassured about what God demanded of him.'[7] He was finally asked, 'Will you retract? Yes or no?' Luther was filled with the Spirit when he replied that unless he were proved wrong on the basis of Scripture and sound reason (for popes and councils had erred and might err again) he was bound fast by his conscience to the word of God. He could not and would not retract. He added, 'May God help me, Amen.' Luther was given a special filling of the Spirit to deal with this situation. He was the recipient of the fulfilment of the promise of the Lord, 'The Holy Spirit will teach you in that very hour what you ought to say' (*Luke* 12:11). God may thus

[7] James Atkinson, *Martin Luther and the Birth of Protestantism* (London: Marshall, Morgan and Scott, 1982) p. 201.

meet his servants in such crises, and fill them with his Spirit. This is absolutely indispensable. We cannot advance against the tide of anti-Christian ideology without such outpourings. However, such fullness cannot be stored up. When men enter the pulpit to preach the Word, they must cultivate an ever-increasing dependence upon the Holy Spirit, and look to him for an enabling beyond their own powers.

So, then, Luke introduces us to Philip. He had become a Christian by the Holy Spirit's regenerating work which had affected every aspect of his being, and in that sense, therefore, Philip was full of the Spirit. His whole status was irreversibly changed. Then Philip matured so that his growth in grace was evident to all, the entire congregation being able to see that he was a strong and wise believer, one who was 'full of the Spirit'. They proceeded to set him aside for the work of ministering to the elderly widows in the congregation. Then, through the onset of persecution, Philip left Jerusalem and went to Samaria where the Holy Spirit was poured out upon him so that he 'proclaimed the Christ there' (*Acts* 8:5) resulting in much joy flooding that city (*Acts* 8:8). This was a special outpouring of the Holy Spirit for a particular sovereign work of grace. Christ poured out his Spirit on that city in Samaria just as he had poured out that same Spirit upon Jerusalem under Peter preaching; but, in Samaria, the preacher was Philip.

So in conclusion I have three things to say:

1. If you are without Christ, then you have the most urgent and incalculable need of God the Holy Spirit. If you are going to believe upon the Lord Jesus Christ, turning from your sins to live a new and godly life you must

be born of the Spirit from above. He can change every part of you. Your great duty is to cry mightily to God, 'Create in me a clean heart O God!' (*Psa.* 51:10). Do not stop until you know by experience that God has answered your cry.

2. If you are a follower of Jesus Christ, then the Scriptures command you to go on being filled with the Spirit. Let every part of your life come under the sway of the word of our Lord Jesus Christ so that you are able to serve the Lord and care for your fellow believers in the church.

3. If you are concerned for the name of Jesus Christ, do not bewail the fact that congregations are in decline and do not complain about the day of small things. Do not forget about the one great divine remedy – the Holy Spirit. What we need more of is his presence, his comfort, and the courage he provides. We stand in need of his energizing and enabling power. He gives life where there is death and Christlikeness where there is sin. It is not enough to know that there are problems and to be able to analyse them carefully. We must get hold of the great remedy for all our infirmities – the outpouring of the Holy Spirit upon God's people. Whether you call such divine visitations 'baptisms', 'fillings', or 'anointings', it does not really matter. The actual phrases are not so important as the meaning and the reality they convey, which is all-important for the glory of God and the growth of the church.

2

THE PLACE GOD SENT HIM

*Philip went down to the city of Samaria and proclaimed
to them the Christ (Acts 8:5).*

Philip was a mature Christian, that is, he was 'full of
the Spirit and of wisdom' (*Acts* 6:3). Moreover,
through a special enabling of the Spirit he had a brief but
extraordinary awakening ministry in Samaria. The history of this 'revival' in Samaria offers lessons about what
kind of preaching God uses to save sinners. But, first, let
us think about the place where Philip went.

1. WHERE PHILIP WENT

The land of Israel was divided into three areas. In the north
there was Galilee. Here we find Nazareth where Jesus was
brought up, the beautiful Sea of Galilee where Peter, James,
and John had their fishing business, and Capernaum and
Bethsaida where much of Jesus' early ministry took place.
Then, to the south lay the area of Judea, in which Jerusalem and Bethlehem are located. Between Galilee in the north
and Judea in the south lay the third area of ancient Israel,
Samaria. This region stretched from the Mediterranean
coast in the west about forty miles across to the river
Jordan in the east. From north to south it was about thirty

miles long. Its capital city was also called Samaria – though Herod the Great had its name changed to Sebastos. Samaria was about the size of a small country, covering an area of approximately twelve hundred square miles. Galilee was about the same size, but Judea, which had the capital, was twice as large.

The territory of Israel was a long narrow land scarcely more than fifty miles wide anywhere. Stretching right across the middle of this land was Samaria. If anyone wished to travel from Judea in the south to Galilee in the north then, other than crossing the Jordan and travelling along the trans-Jordan route, one had to pass through Samaria. Many of the devout Old Testament believers who lived in Galilee travelled through Samaria to attend the annual feasts of Passover, Pentecost, and Tabernacles in Jerusalem.

What made Samaria different from Judea and why was it that the Jews had no dealings with the Samaritans? The reasons for this sad state of affairs stretch back a thousand years before the time of Philip the evangelist! After king Solomon's reign the united kingdom of Israel split into two parts, with the ten northern tribes breaking away from Judah and Benjamin under the leadership of Jeroboam I. Two tribes remained loyal to the Davidic dynasty at Jerusalem. The ten northern tribes made their capital at Samaria. Their subsequent history was one of theological and cultural backsliding and declension. The Northern Kingdom was captured by Assyria in 722 BC and thousands of Samaria's Israelites were deported to foreign lands, while many foreign people were taken from their own territories and forcibly resettled in Samaria. Even the northern region of Galilee became known as

'Galilee of the Gentiles'. Much inter-marrying between the peoples of these nations took place. The newcomers looked on Yahweh as being no more than the local deity of Samaria. There is a fascinating paragraph describing this set of affairs in 2 Kings, telling us that 'every nation still made gods of its own and put them in the shrines of the high places that the Samaritans had made . . . they feared the LORD but also served their own gods, after the manner of the nations from among whom they had been carried away' (2 *Kings* 17:29, 33). All this was going on in the very land that God had promised to give to his own people. Some years later, when the people of Judah returned from their own seventy years of exile in Babylon and began to rebuild the city and the temple, the people of Samaria made an offer to help them. But the Jews of Jerusalem, fresh from their exile in Babylon had been stung by God's punishment for their own idolatrous ways, and were offended by the religious compromise of the Samaritans. They would not accept any help from them whatsoever.

Two hundred years later the Samaritans built a temple on Mount Gerizim to rival the temple of Yahweh in Jerusalem. The Samaritans also rejected the Old Testament Scriptures, except for the five books of Moses. They did this because their view of history forced them to reject the prophecies that spoke about the coming of the Messiah from the line of David. For them prophecy ended with Moses and would find its fulfilment in another prophet like Moses whom God would raise up and through whom God would restore all things.

Later still, while the Maccabees in Jerusalem resisted the religious oppression of the Syrian despot Antiochus

IV in 167 BC and suffered torture rather than surrender, the Samaritans capitulated and readily rededicated their temple to the Greek god Zeus. So the Jews, who saw the Samaritans as schismatics, compromisers, and heretics, despised them and their syncretistic[1] religion. This is why the Jews had no dealings with the Samaritans (*John* 4:9). The Samaritans were basically in the same category as Gentiles; they were outsiders and did not belong to the house of Israel. The division was sharp and bitter; a Jew would not even drink from a Samaritan cup. Indeed, only a very unconventional Jew would ask for water from a Samaritan woman and allow his lips to touch the edge of her cup. So a deep chasm divided these two peoples. A Jew could dismiss someone he deplored with the words – 'You are a Samaritan' (see *John* 8:48).

In the Gospels we read about the Lord Jesus and his disciples visiting a Samaritan village. The villagers rejected their message, and James and John asked the Lord if the time had not come for divine vengeance to fall upon them. Was not he the prophesied One who would baptize with fire and the Holy Spirit? 'Call down condemnation from heaven and destroy these heretics!' the 'Sons of Thunder' cried. The Lord rebuked them (*Luke* 9:52–55). Did Jesus not heal ten lepers? And yet the only one who returned to give God thanks was a Samaritan (*Luke* 17:11–19). Jesus also told the parable of the Good Samaritan, and how the Jewish priest and Levite hurried past the badly beaten man lying at the side of the road, showing him no compassion whatsoever. The only person to stop and help him was a Samaritan (*Luke* 10:30–37). We also read of a time when a constraint was once laid upon the Lord to

---

[1] *Syncretistic:* blending or fusing religions together.

go through the land of Samaria, and there, at Jacob's well in Sychar, he met a Samaritan woman. She was acutely aware of the deep division between their two nations, and in many ways she was a typical Samaritan, for she knew something of the religious history of Samaria and Judea, and was willing to debate religious doctrines. And yet, at the very same time, she was living an immoral life, having had five husbands, and currently living with another man who was not her husband. As Jesus spoke to this sinful woman her ears and heart opened to his message. She was transformed by the Jew she met by the well and immediately brought other Samaritans to hear him. Many men and women of Sychar came to see Jesus and begged him to stay with them a little while longer. For two days he taught them and many more Samaritans believed because of his own word (*John* 4:4–43).

So Samaria was a mission field, on the very doorstep of Israel, and formed something of a natural bridge to the whole Gentile and pagan world.

2. WHY PHILIP WENT

Why did Philip go to Samaria? He did not go to Samaria because he was sure that there was going to be a revival or a wonderful response to the gospel. Although the Lord had stirred the village of Sychar during that brief but memorable visit, the Twelve had had no response from their foray into Samaria. They returned to Israel angry and frustrated. Philip could have had no inkling that there was going to be a revival in Samaria. He had no more conviction of a great awakening happening there than Paul had when he visited Thessalonica, Corinth, or Ephesus. Nor was it that Philip was getting better as a 'deacon' and relished a new challenge – progressing from serving tables to addressing these northern heretics. We are not informed that he had ever preached publicly before going to Samaria. Neither did he go out of any feeling of kinship with or natural affection for the Samaritans. Quite the reverse; any change of heart he had towards the Samaritans was the result of the grace of Christ at work within him.

Why, then, did Philip go to that nation and proclaim Christ to them? There is only one answer: the Lord Jesus told the church to 'preach the gospel to every creature'. When Jesus began his ministry he had gone primarily to the 'lost sheep of the house of Israel', and he had told the disciples not to go to Samaria, but to concentrate upon Israel. Following his resurrection a new international dispensation began for the church and the Word of God went out from Zion in ever increasing circles to the uttermost parts of the earth. Jesus said to his disciples, 'You will be my witnesses in . . . Samaria' (*Acts* 1:8). Just after speaking those words he was taken up from before his disciples into heaven. Is it not the case that the last words we hear from our dearest loved ones are very precious to us? The fact that Jesus left this earth with the word 'Samaria' upon his lips would have been important to Philip, even if he was not among that select group of disciples who stood on the Mount of Ascension to hear them. 'Go and speak of me in Samaria', the disciples had been told. The command of Christ to preach the gospel to all men is the all-sufficient mandate we have to evangelize the world. 'Make disciples of all nations', the Lord commanded, 'and do not forget about Samaria.' Why must we take the message of the Lord Jesus outside the confines of the church? Why must we go to people who have no knowledge of Jesus Christ, who often think in terms of 'another gospel' (which is no gospel at all), and who live in utter hostility to our message? Because the Lord Jesus Christ has told us to 'Go into all the world.' In the light of Christ's word there is no place for racial prejudice within Christ's church. What if the unreached belong to a country that dropped an atomic bomb on your grandparents? What if they are of that tribe whose members set alight the vehicle in which a missionary and his two sons were sleeping? What if they belong to that religion which persecuted with horrible tortures your fore-fathers four hundred years ago? 'Go into all the world'!

The Serbian Christian must preach the gospel of free grace to the Albanian Muslim. The converted Catholic Irishman must preach that same gospel to the unconverted Protestant Ulsterman. Philip did not know whether God was going to save many or few of the people of Samaria, but he knew that he lived his life under the authority of Christ. Christ had commanded that his disciples must go to Samaria and preach to everyone who will listen to them everything about himself – whatsoever he had taught them (*Matt.* 28:19–20).

3. WHEN PHILIP WENT

Philip went because of Christ's missionary mandate, but he went at that particular time because the stoning of his friend Stephen had stirred up a blood lust among the Jews of Jerusalem. On the day of Stephen's martyrdom 'a great persecution arose against the church at Jerusalem, and they were all scattered throughout the regions of Judea and Samaria except the apostles' (*Acts* 8:1). Philip saw the high cost of serving the Lord in Stephen's death. He, too, might have to lay down his life for his Saviour.

While Philip and a large number of other Christians fled Jerusalem to escape prison, torture, and death, the martyrdom of Stephen would doubtless have strengthened their evangelistic zeal. Who would not have been stirred by hearing Stephen's final sermon, and seeing his face like 'the face of an angel' (*Acts* 6:15)? His last words were full of tenderness and compassion, yet full of power and glory. He said, 'Behold I see the heavens opened and the Son of man standing at the right hand of God . . . Lord Jesus receive my spirit . . . Lord, do not hold this sin against them' (*Acts* 7:56, 59, 60). Only a man full of the Holy Spirit could speak like that. Can you imagine what must it have been like to have stood there and to have heard your closest friend speak such words before sealing his testimony with his blood? After Stephen's death there could be no half-measures in the disciples' commitment to and service of the Lord. Philip was on his way to Samaria with a gospel that enabled men to bear witness to the truth and die like Stephen! All the world must hear this gospel!

John Wesley said, 'Our people die well.' To die well is a great and blessed thing. But there is only one way you can die well, and that is to live well. Only the Spirit of the Lord Jesus can empower a person to both live and die well.

The great persecution of Christ's people in England and Wales in the mid-sixteenth century under Queen Mary when hundreds of people were burned alive at the stake demonstrated this very truth; Christ's people die well. That period saw the first great awakening in Britain, and created an evangelistic flood that swept the gospel through the length and breadth of a barren land. Christian people, who spoke so articulately before their judges and died with such assurance and peace, possessed something that hundreds of others began to want for themselves. God blessed the persecution of his people to establish and strengthen the cause of the gospel in Britain. 'The blood of the martyrs is the seed of the church', or to change the metaphor, 'The wind increases the flame.'

The persecution that arose in Jerusalem after Stephen's death was used by the Lord to drive his people out from Jerusalem. God has his own sovereign ways of constraining his people to obey his commands. The salt was still in the salt-cellar and the time had come for it to be scattered abroad to season and preserve a decaying world of sin. The light was in danger of being put under a bushel in Jerusalem and God was going to take the hammer of persecution to break the bushel and let the light shine out in all its glory. The Lord continues to open up new ways to prevent the church from keeping the gospel within its comfortable confines. In 1949 the Communists defeated the corrupt National Government of China. Six hundred and thirty-seven missionaries working with the China Inland Mission were deported from the country. Within four years almost half of them had been redeployed in South-East Asia and Japan. Back in China the national church grew remarkably and is now estimated to be forty times the size it was fifty years ago when the missionaries were expelled. Opposition and persecution helped to spread the gospel through much of South-East Asia.

4. HOW PHILIP WENT
As a Herald Clothed with Divine Authority
Philip went to Samaria with a sense of *divine authority*.

We are told, 'Philip went down to the city of Samaria and proclaimed to them the Christ' (*Acts* 8:5). The word 'proclaimed' means 'heralded'. It is the first time in the book of Acts that Luke uses this particular term to describe the preaching of the gospel. The New Testament preacher is a herald, a man authorized by the King of heaven to take his Prince's message to the whole world. He must make a public proclamation telling mankind that their great Creator-King has a message for them.

The herald declares this word to elicit the response of obedience. This is not an invitation to a 'chat-line' on some fascinating issue; God calls upon men to change their ways as a result of the message declared by his herald. The preacher is aware of this authority that his Master has invested him with. He must deliver the message exactly as he has received it. He dare not make his own modifications to the King's words. He is an ambassador of the King of kings. This is the great title the apostle Paul uses to describe a preacher of the gospel in 2 Corinthians 5:18–21 – 'We are ambassadors for Christ.' When John Venn was ordained to the Christian ministry in 1782 Charles Simeon wrote a letter congratulating him, 'not on a permission to receive £40 or £50 a year, nor on the title of Reverend, but on your accession to the most valuable, most honourable, most important, and most glorious office in the world – to that of an ambassador of the Lord Jesus Christ.' Oh, how the Christian church needs to recapture this high view of the preaching ministry!

So Philip came to Samaria and heralded the Christ, the Messiah. This must have brought him into conflict with the Samaritan religion, for their understanding of the Messiah was very different from the message Philip declared. They were expecting a special prophet like Moses, and little more. Having rejected the Psalms and the Prophets the Samaritans were ignorant of Isaiah's great description of Yahweh's suffering Servant, and David's portrayal of Israel's suffering King. Their faith was crippled by a doctrine of limited inspiration. Philip came to tell them that the Christ was indeed of the line of David and was born in Bethlehem.

He had to tell them of how in these latter days the prophecies of the Jewish Scriptures had been wonderfully fulfilled in Jesus. The Samaritans had been stumbling along with an abridged Bible. They had virtually torn out and discarded large sections of the Word of God. Consequently, their religion was impoverished, as are all religions that ignore what God has communicated to mankind. There was no avoiding the necessity of charging their consciences with this neglect, and urging a thorough-going reformation of their religion. The herald's message demands a change, even if all Samaria says, 'Who does he think he is? He thinks he is right and everyone else is wrong.' Let not the preacher be intimidated by men: let him serve his King and faithfully deliver the King's message.

The Christian gospel is a message of authority, and before any appeal is made to respond to it people must first feel the power of its truth on their lives, demanding their total submission. The gospel is a declaration to men and women that the long-promised Messiah has come, and it points to everything that he has taught and achieved. The One whose voice the wind and waves obeyed, and before whose Name demons cringed in fear, now addresses men and women through his gospel heralds. Their preaching is invested with all the power and authority of the Godhead. Through their preaching Christ's call is heard: 'Come unto me all you that labour and are heavy-laden and I will give you rest.' This is the King bidding men come to him. Down from your tree, Zacchaeus! Away from the your seat at the tax-collecting booth, Matthew! Away from your fishing boats, Peter and John! Follow me, and I will make you fishers of men. The King of heaven comes in the form of his ambassador-heralds and now speaks to everyone.

God does not negotiate with the Samaritans in Philip's message. He has not sent his servant there to open up a dialogue. The King of kings declares a word that requires Samaritan compliance. Let these rebels lay down their arms. The spirit of the gospel demands a communication that, while not loud and bombastic, is yet authoritative in its tone: 'The Messiah has come and has spoken. He has died and has risen again, and now it is time for you to respond.' Philip went to the Samaritan people urging acceptance of and surrender to his message. It was not arrogant of Philip to consider himself a herald of the King of heaven. He was his herald indeed. Philip was little concerned about what the Samaritans' would think of him, or even of their opinion of Jesus Christ. Instead, Philip was consumed with the honour and glory of the One he served. He came to Samaria conscious that he was publishing a message that did not have its origin in his own imagination but that had been given to him by his King.

In 1743 a shipwright by the name of John Tanner went to hear George Whitefield preach in Plymouth, intending to knock the renowned preacher off his platform. But as Whitefield began to declare the gospel Tanner was astonished at what he heard and could not go a step further in his sinful ways. Then, suddenly, the preacher turned in Tanner's direction and looked him full in the face and cried out, 'Sinner, thou art the man that crucified the Son of God.' At that very moment, Tanner felt a sword piercing his soul and broke down in tears. All his arrogance was destroyed in an instant and he humbly fell before the One whom his sins had crucified. That day Tanner received and rested upon Jesus Christ, the Saviour of sinners. In George Whitefield we see a wonderful example of the authority with which Christ's heralds are clothed as they boldly declare their Master's Word. A great awakening began in Samaria when Philip heralded the Word of God.

We need to be more aware of the authority that rests upon the preachers whom our Lord has called. We should not see them as men with pleasing personalities and wonderful gifts of communication. Instead, we ought to see them as men on a heavenly mission and clothed with divine authority. There is something unusual and different about them, a sense of God that ultimately comes from their being personally called by him to be the heralds of his message. The other elders and officers in the church do not have that particular calling. They are not the Lord's heralds as the preacher is, even though they do possess true gifts of leadership and the ministry of mercy. A congregation ought to recognize the unique call of the pastor-teacher when it assembles for worship. How few of today's worship-leaders who come to the rostrum to do 'their thing' exercise the gifts of God in the way that the Spirit-anointed herald does whom God has appointed to preach forth his Word. If the truth be told, the Spirit is

quenched when the natural talents of voice and music de-
tract from the herald's divine vocation. The herald should
not have to battle against an atmosphere of excitement
engineered by the power of the flesh. It is surely an evi-
dence of the Spirit's absence that men and women feel they
must work something up in order to compensate for the
power vacuum in their gatherings for worship. Where is
that sense of awe that marked the presence of the Spirit of
God in the early church (*Acts* 2:43)?

With a Message of Good News

Secondly, Philip went to Samaria with a message of *good
news:* 'Philip . . . preached good news' (*Acts* 8:12). Preaching the good news does not merely refer to the preaching
of sermons by the church's pastor. We are told that all the
believers who fled from Jerusalem preached the word
wherever they went (*Acts* 8:4). This is the same word as
is subsequently used to describe Philip's work in Samaria
– the whole church had good news to preach to the world.

And what good news it was! How different was the
commission the prophet Jonah received from the Lord –
'Arise, go to Nineveh, that great city, and call out against
it, for their evil has come up before me' (*Jon.* 1:2). When
the prophet eventually arrived in the community to which
he was sent, he cried to them, 'Yet forty days, and Nineveh
shall be overthrown!' (*Jon.* 3:4). There was no good news
for them! And yet the Ninevites said to one another, 'Who
knows what might happen if we cry to God for mercy?'
In fact, through the mercy of God, salvation was given to
them and a city was transformed by the grace of God.
But the message to Samaria was good news from the
beginning. Does this mean that Samaria was morally

better or much more deserving of God's favour than Nineveh? No, it does not mean that at all! The gospel to the Samaritans reminds us of the words Jesus spoke, that in these last days, 'God did not send his Son into the world to condemn the world, but in order that the world might be saved through him' (*John* 3:17).

The gospel is good news – the message of what God has done for sinners in his Son, Jesus Christ. This good news looks back to something great that happened in the past. 'For God so loved the world that he gave his only Son' (*John* 3:16). This news is all about an historical event that had its origin in the great love of God. The good news that Philip preached to the Samaritans was all about the coming into the world of the Messiah, a man known as Jesus of Nazareth. On a specific day in the past a young virgin woman found herself pregnant and when her time was come she gave birth to a baby boy and gave him the name 'Jesus'. On another day thirty-three years later, this same Person was unlawfully put to death by crucifixion on a hill outside the city of Jerusalem. On the third day after his death and burial he physically rose from the dead, and was seen during a period lasting forty days by various people on different occasions and in a number of locations. Shortly after, he ascended bodily into heaven. The good news is all about One who lived and died in this very real world. In other words, it is not a myth. These events did not occur in a fantasy world like C. S. Lewis's Narnia, but in our own needy world – planet Earth. At first the eyewitnesses exclusively spoke about these historical facts, but later they wrote them down in four Gospels, a book of Acts, and in Letters. Huge numbers of people from all sorts of backgrounds believed the good news through the testimony of the men who had been Jesus' companions and friends.

The church has a message of good news for all. The humblest Christian can stand before the most wicked and debauched sinner this world has ever seen and say, with all the authority of God and with the utmost sincerity, 'I have good news for you. I know One who can save you. Though your sins are like scarlet, though your past is stained by sin and your present is horribly compromised, and though death and hell lie before you, I have good news about Jesus Christ, the Saviour of the world.' That is good news indeed! 'Come from your unbelief and your sin and turn to this Saviour who is ready to receive you just as you are.' There can be no spiritual awakenings without preachers being persuaded of the goodness of this good news.

With Good News about a Person

Thirdly, Philip went to Samaria with good news about a *Person*. 'Philip . . . proclaimed to them the Christ' (*Acts* 8:5). Later in the chapter we read that Philip told the Ethiopian 'the good news about Jesus' (*Acts* 8:35). Significantly, to the Samaritans Philip preached 'Christ', the Messiah, the Anointed One of God, the long promised One who in these last days was revealed to men. To the Ethiopian reading about Yahweh's Suffering Servant from Isaiah chapter 53 Philip preached 'Jesus' thus identifying the mysterious person of Isaiah 53 to the curious African. When we are told that Philip preached 'Jesus' and 'Christ' it goes without saying that Philip's priority was not to take the law of God and preach that to the Samaritans or the Ethiopian. They already had the law, believing it to be written by the finger of God. It was the One who had come to fulfil the law about whom they needed to hear.

Today the church is under pressure to make the righteous law of God its priority. We see moral declension all around and feel constrained to declare, perhaps in a rather unbalanced manner, God's holy demands to a hurting people. That has always been a temptation to preachers. Daniel Rowland began his ministry on this kind of 'legal' note. One of his biographers says:

> What he preached at first was the law, in its high and minute demands, and in its awful threatenings. He stood, as it were, on Mount Sinai, and loudly proclaimed eternal perdition to a sinful world. Awful and extremely terrific was his message; nothing but the consuming flashes and dreadful thunders of the law, with hardly anything like the joyful sounds of the Gospel.[2]

People were broken and convicted by his messages, but little more than that. His people felt greatly convicted of their sin, but did not feel the great joy that Jesus alone brings. Then another minister who was also named Philip – Philip Pugh – approached Rowland and gave him some advice: 'Preach the Gospel to the people, dear Sir, and apply the balm of Gilead, the blood of Christ, to their spiritual wounds, and show the necessity of faith in the crucified Saviour.' Rowland said to him, 'I am afraid that I have not that faith myself in its vigour and full exercise.' Then Philip Pugh replied, 'Preach on it till you feel it in that way; no doubt it will come. If you go on preaching the law in this manner, you will kill half the people in the country.' In the same way Samaria heard Philip presenting to them, not the law, but the good news of this glorious person, Jesus the Messiah.

The Christian faith is about receiving the Lord Jesus Christ into our lives. It is not about mentally embracing a set of facts about Jesus that we have gleaned from a course of study. Is marriage only accepting certain important facts about a member of the opposite sex? In a wedding ceremony does the officiating minister say to the bride, 'Will you receive these details as true about this man?' No! She is asked if she will take him to herself as her lawfully wedded husband. So it is with a true receiving of Christ: Philip can show who the Messiah is and tell the Samaritans all about the life, teaching, miraculous works, death, and resurrection of Christ, but that is not enough to save any single one of them. They must receive Christ into their lives as Lord and Saviour; then everything changes.

It was Jesus Christ, introduced to these Samaritans by Philip's preaching, who transformed their lives and renewed their minds, hearts, and lifestyles. Philip saw this accomplished as he told them everything he had learned about the Person and work of Christ. His message was Christ-centred.

With a Message about a Kingdom

Fourthly, Philip went to Samaria with a message about a *kingdom:* 'Philip . . . preached good news about the kingdom of God' (*Acts* 8:12). God has a domain, a sphere of influence over which he reigns. He has subjects who obey him, all of whom he protects with impregnable walls of salvation. The Father has made his Christ the King of this kingdom. Before Jesus ascended into heaven he said, 'All authority in heaven and on earth has been given to me.'

Think of the three symbols of the good news of Jesus: a cradle, a cross and a crown. He was uniquely born of a virgin. He, like no other, died as an utterly sinless man bearing the sins of others. He is now the exalted King of heaven and Lord of the Universe. He became King by only one route, via the womb of Mary, the suffering of Calvary, the deadness of the tomb, and the victory of the resurrection. The same Person who lived among men now rules as King over the nations. He becomes the King of favoured men and women at the same time as he becomes their Saviour. None of the benefits of his forgiveness are given to them without the simultaneous extension of his lordship over them. If men take the blessings of pardon from an offended God they must also take the responsibilities of belonging to King Jesus. Can you imagine a God who would come by his Holy Spirit and join to Christ one single person who had no intention of loving and serving his Son – placing someone 'in Christ' who rejects Christ's Lordship?

Unthinkable! Rather, by that same act of uniting the sinner to Christ, God, by his Spirit, renews the sinner's heart and fills it with longing for a new way of life. 'Let all the house of Israel know for certain, that God has made him both Lord and Christ, this Jesus whom you crucified' (*Acts* 2:36). 'If you confess with your mouth that Jesus is Lord and believe in your heart that God raised him from the dead, you will be saved' (*Rom.* 10:9). 'Believe in the Lord Jesus Christ and you will be saved' (*Acts* 16:31). Christ is not merely a forgiving 'Friend of sinners'; he is also Master of his disciples, whose Word they lovingly obey. It is the *Lord* Jesus Christ who saves us. It is King Jesus who saves us from our sins. So faith in an uncrowned Saviour is not to be equated with a genuine faith in the Jesus Christ of Scripture. Faith in a Jesus who does not resemble the Jesus of Scripture will save no one. Faithful pastors will never play down the demands of Christ's kingdom in order to keep unbelievers happy or add them to the church's roll-book. Evangelical preachers will proclaim the whole gospel, the one given to us by the King of kings.

There is hardly a Bible-believing minister who does not recognize that the church needs to be revived. But it is a fact that revivals often take place at the same time as many churchgoers become convinced that, in spite of appearances, they are not truly born again. Disobedience rather than whole-hearted obedience to the commands of Christ has characterized their lives, and upon making such a disturbing discovery they cry, 'Men and brethren, what shall we do?' Our rejection of Christ's kingship is sinful and has the effect of quenching the Spirit of revival. The preaching of Jesus Christ is the great means of motivating men and women to the joyful obedience that flows from faith in Jesus.

With a Verbal Message

Fifthly, Philip brought this message to them *in words*. All the believers who were scattered by the persecution went about 'preaching the word' (*Acts* 8:4). Philip was no exception, and 'the apostles in Jerusalem heard that Samaria had accepted the word of God' (*Acts* 8:14). When Peter and John came to Samaria they did the same: they 'testified and spoke the word of the Lord' (*Acts* 8:25).

The mighty acts of God are related to us in words. They have their own specific logic and rationality. God does not communicate with us through goose-bumps, visions, and out-of-body experiences; he communicates to us by words. When Philip came to Samaria his one weapon was 'the sword of the Spirit, which is the word of God' (*Eph.* 6:17). When Paul wanted to strengthen troubled Christians in Thessalonica he wrote two epistles to them, in one of which he said, 'Comfort one another with these words.' Words from one person to another are crucial. All of us are what we are today through words.

'The Preacher sought to find words of delight, and uprightly he wrote words of truth.' Such 'words of the wise', especially when they combine grace and truth, are 'like goads' that prick the conscience and stimulate the mind. They are also 'like nails firmly fixed' because they lodge in the memory and are not easily unfastened (*Eccles.* 12:10–11). It is worth taking trouble over words. Have something to say, and say it as clearly as you can. People need plain speaking.

C. S. Lewis once wrote a letter to a teenager in America in which he gave sound advice about plain speaking. His main points were these:

1. Always try to use the language that will make quite clear what you mean, and make sure your sentence couldn't mean anything else.

2. Always prefer the plain, direct word to the long vague one. Don't 'implement' promises, but 'keep' them.

3. Never use abstract nouns when concrete ones will do. If you mean 'more people died', don't say 'mortality rose'.

4. Don't use adjectives that merely tell us how you want us to feel about the thing you are describing. I mean, instead of telling us a thing was 'terrible', describe it so we'll be terrified. Don't say it was 'delightful'; make us say 'delightful' when we've read the description. You see, all those words (*horrifying, wonderful, hideous, exquisite*) are only saying to your readers 'please will you do my job for me'.

5. Don't use words too big for the subject. 'Don't say "infinitely" when you mean "very": otherwise you'll have no word left when you want to talk about something really infinite.[3]

J. C. Ryle has an address worthy of constant re-reading entitled, 'Simplicity in Preaching'.[4] His five headings are:

1. If you want to attain simplicity in preaching, you must have a clear knowledge of what you are going to preach.

2. You must use simple words.

3. You must seek to acquire a simple style of composition, with short sentences and as few colons and semicolons as possible.

4. You must aim at directness.

5. You must make an abundant use of illustration and anecdote.

'Aim at directness', says Ryle, and, oh, how he excelled in this himself! Another fine example of directness in speech

[3] C. S. Lewis, *Letters*, p. 271.
[4] J. C. Ryle, *The Upper Room* (1888; repr. London: Banner of Truth, 1970) pp. 35-55.

was the Puritan preacher and author Joseph Alleine. Al Martin makes the following comments about the style of writing in Alleine's book, *A Sure Guide to Heaven:*[5]

> Again and again Alleine backs the sinner against the wall, as it were, with questions which cause the sinner to reflect upon his way, upon his own state before God. He will ask him, 'Are you at peace? Show me upon what grounds your peace is maintained. Is it a spiritual peace? Can you show the distinguishing marks of a sound believer? Can you evidence something more than any hypocrite in the world ever had? If not, fear this peace more than any trouble, and know that a carnal peace commonly proves to be the most mortal enemy of the soul. Whilst it kisses and smiles fairly, it fatally smites, as it were, under the fifth rib. Now conscience, do your work, speak out.'[6]

So Philip went armed with words. There was to be no dimming of the lights, no playing of soft music, no cleverness in speech, no persuasive words of wisdom, no techniques of communication that might elicit some change of mood or favourable response. The good news must capture the hearts of the Samaritans, not the eloquence of the preacher. You might well think, how could Philip realistically expect his gospel to succeed without all these rhetorical techniques? His expectation was centred on God. He looked to heaven and relied upon the power and blessing of God upon his Word. He prayed that the Holy Spirit would supernaturally assure his hearers of the divine truth of the gospel.

[5] Joseph Alleine, *A Sure Guide to Heaven* (1671; repr. London: Banner of Truth, 1959).
[6] A. N. Martin, *What's Wrong With Preaching Today?* (Edinburgh: Banner of Truth, 1967) p. 23.

As a Preacher with Power

Sixthly, Philip went as one who wrought *mighty works*. 'And the crowds with one accord paid attention to what was being said by Philip when they heard him and saw the signs that he did. For unclean spirits came out of many who were possessed, crying with a loud voice, and many who were paralysed or lame were healed' (*Acts* 8:7). We are told that Simon Magus was 'amazed' by the 'signs and great miracles' (*Acts* 8:13).

Let us imagine that a man comes knocking on my door and introduces himself to me as a gospel preacher, and telling me that he would like to do some open-air preaching in our town centre. I would ask him something about his beliefs to discover his soundness and orthodoxy, and then I would ask him if he had any letters of reference; without good references I could not give him my support. Should he give me names of men I esteem, I would phone them and make some inquiries. Let us say that they tell me that he is a fine preacher whom the Lord has blessed with an awakening ministry. He has preached in their churches, and they envy my privilege of having him in our own town. They tell of some of the things that happened when he visited them, and my heart begins to beat in expectation. So I tell the man that I am glad he is going to preach in the town and ask him when he would like to start. 'This afternoon', he says.

So, later that afternoon he goes down to the middle of the town and begins to preach. He really is like no other street preacher I have heard. His ministry is lucid, arresting, convicting, persuasive, and soon he has a crowd of people listening to him. Soon we invite him to preach every day in our church building and many are drawn to hear him. By the first Sunday he is able to draw a large number of people to church who are gripped by his preaching. Many flock to the prayer meeting and there is a long queue to get into church on Sunday morning and evening.

Such a phenomenon is so rare that I have to confess that I have never heard such a thing happening in living memory. But this is how I envisage a Spirit-filled man with an awakening ministry behaving today.

In our imaginary scenario let us go one step further. One day he is with a blind man, a well-known character around the town, and suddenly he cries that he can now see perfectly. A handicapped person in a wheelchair leaps up and begins to walk for the first time in his life. The preacher then calls on a dear sister who is dying of cancer and has just a few weeks of her life on earth left. He reads the Scriptures and prays and before he leaves the room she appears to have been miraculously cured of her disease. A man who had been deaf for fifty years can suddenly hear again. The preacher goes to the home for mentally handicapped people and he heals every single one of them – including the Downs' Syndrome men and women who are completely restored. Someone who has never been able to speak properly is now quite articulate.

Then a grieving mother takes him to a funeral parlour and shows him the little coffin in which her young daughter lies who was killed in a traffic accident just three days earlier. The funeral service is due to take place the following day. Without any fuss, he prays, then takes her hand, and raises her to life, while the undertaker tears up the death certificate! If such a man came to town we would gladly welcome him and rejoice in his God-given preaching gifts. If he should have the additional gift of performing miracles I would not be the one saying to him, 'You shouldn't be doing that sort of thing. That was a gift which authenticated the apostles and which has since been withdrawn.' None of us would grumble to be witnesses of a truly apostolic miraculous ministry. We would be rejoicing in our deaf brother being able to hear, and our Downs' Syndrome brother and sister being healed, and our sister cured of cancer, and the dead raised to life. No one is going to oppose *real* miracles which have been done by a reputable servant of the Lord Jesus Christ, are they? Everyone would be too full of praise to God.

All of us would have to agree that these would be extraordinary miracles. But let us go one necessary step further in our imaginary scenario. Now that all in our town have heard of this preacher, the news has quickly spread throughout Wales and beyond. Every person suffering from an incurable illness is being transported from a wide area and ushered to the evangelist for healing. Queues of sick and dying people have formed outside his house by 5.30 a.m.! The crowds still gather to hear him, but are now not really paying very close attention to what he is preaching. They want healing, not preaching! He has healed others, he must heal them and their loved ones too. They become insistent and demanding. It is said that people are coming from Sweden, and even as far away as Brazil! E-mails are being sent from country to country right around the world. Reporters fill the town's guesthouses and hotels. The pressures on our preacher mount and become so great that he finally moves to another town and even appeals that his whereabouts be kept hidden. Now there is resentment that he did not stay longer and heal all the sick folk in the town. Many become embittered. They have spent a lot of money and have travelled far. Their children are dying and he has gone into hiding! There is uproar. Do you see what has happened? The miracles have become a hindrance to this blessed man's preaching of a free and eternal salvation in the Lord Jesus Christ.

Of course, this is all just an imaginary scenario. We all know that things like these do not happen today, and indeed, have not happened since the closing of the New Testament period signalled by the death of Christ's apostles. But the reality facing us presents us with a very different set of problems that lead us to do two things.

Firstly, we feel we must oppose every man who claims he can do miracles but whose claims cannot be verified and whose healing services are performed in a show-business, carnal, and manipulative manner – with fake healings, appeals for money, and all the jiggery-pokery of modern 'faith-healers'. Such men are a disgrace and bring the glorious name of our Lord Jesus Christ into disrepute. Their behaviour and unverifiable claims betray the absence of the *Holy* Spirit. We are right to protest when sick people continue to suffer from the same illnesses of which they were supposedly healed. We are right to be critical when the dying are chided for not having enough faith to be healed. How cruel it is to bring such a charge to a sick or dying patient! Such self-confessed healers are charlatans and not the Lord's true servants. The Lord warned us about false teachers, impostors, and wolves in sheep's clothing who would devour and not spare the flock. He told us to be on our guard against all such.

The realities of our present age remind us that the gift of miraculous healing has not been present in the church since the days of the apostles. A comparison of the claims for the restoration of apostolic gifts today with the recorded miracles of Christ and his apostles in the New Testament is enough to convince the unprejudiced mind of the spurious nature of such claims. Moreover, the great men of the post-apostolic church such as Martin Luther, John Calvin, John Bunyan, George Whitefield, John Wesley, Howell Harris, Daniel Rowland, Jonathan Edwards, Charles Spurgeon, Robert Murray M'Cheyne, Andrew and Horatius Bonar, and Martyn Lloyd-Jones did not have the gift to perform miracles – even though their ministries were remarkably full of the Holy Spirit and evidently pleasing to God.

Of course, we rejoice when God answers prayer and marvellously restores the health of a loved one to the astonishment of all, including the doctors and surgeons who, like us, feared the worst-case scenario. God hears the prayers of his people and may answer those prayers as he answered the prayers of the apostle Paul for his seriously ill brother and colleague Epaphroditus (*Phil.* 3:27). But miraculous healing as evidenced in the pages of the New Testament is now a thing of the future and we wait patiently for the day of Christ's return when we shall enjoy the full benefits of the age to come, including the full physical transformation of the body.

The miraculous gifts of the New Testament period were closely linked to the prophetic ministry of Jesus Christ, the establishment of his kingdom in the last days of this world, and the office of the apostles. Christ, has supplied us with the New Testament Scriptures through his apostles and some others who were closely associated with them. We know that these writings are the Word of God, not only because they are self-authenticating, and not only because of what they say, but because they come from the hand of those whom God has attested to us as his chosen servants. Just as Elijah was attested as 'a man of God' who spoke the true word of Yahweh on account of the miraculous raising of the widow's son (*1 Kings* 17:24), so the miracles performed by Christ's apostles attested them as the servants of God, their gospel as the word of God, and that the powers of the age to come as having really invaded our world.

Jesus could point to his miracles as signs that the kingdom of God had come upon the generation who had personally witnessed them (*Luke* 11:20). Peter could tell the Jews of Jerusalem that the Jesus he preached 'was a man attested to you by God with mighty works and wonders and signs that God did through him in your midst' (*Acts* 2:22). Likewise, the writer of the letter to the Hebrews reminded his readers of God's great salvation, and adds, 'It was declared at first by the Lord, and it was attested to us by those who heard, while God also bore witness by signs and wonders and various miracles and by gifts of the Holy Spirit distributed according to his will' (*Heb.* 2:4).

God attested the message of the gospel in this way because it was, in a sense, new. It ushered in a new and final phase of redemptive revelation and history. It brought us the Christ and his single sacrifice for sins for all time and brought an end to the Old Covenant arrangements (*Heb.* 10:12; 8:13; 10:9). It ushered in the day of salvation for 'everyone who calls upon the name of the Lord'

(*Acts* 2:21). Since the coming of Christ we live in the period known as the 'last days' (*Heb.* 1:2). We neither need nor expect new revelations of God's will for our salvation. 'What more can he say than to you he has said?' Our gospel has already been divinely attested when it was first proclaimed in the world by Christ and his apostles. Therefore, we do not need, and shall not expect to see miraculous gifts, signs, and wonders like those performed at that unique period of redemptive history.

But secondly, having said all that, we do look for *power* to accompany our preaching and evangelizing! Philip went to Samaria and preached with power – a power that was felt by all those who heard his message. This was more than the power of persuasive words and speech, more than the power of mere human eloquence. The power that attended Philip's preaching in Samaria was nothing less than 'the power of God for salvation' (*Rom.* 1:16). It was a divine, almighty, irresistible power able to accomplish its saving purposes. See how it worked in the lives of these Samaritan people! In what large numbers did they gather to hear the Lord's servant and with what rapt attention did they listen to his preaching! With what earnestness did they put their trust in the Lord Jesus Christ of whom Philip bore witness! And with what joy did they rejoice in their salvation and the grace of God! Did your preaching or personal evangelism meet with a reception like that? How do the people of your neighbourhood or town react when someone brings the gospel to them? Do I need to say anything more about our need for such power to be given to our personal testimony and preaching? Oh that our preaching was filled with the power that Philip and the Samaritans knew!

How can we preach with such power? This can only come from the Lord himself. He is the sovereign Giver of what we need. To him we must look and to him we must earnestly pray.

Of this the apostle Paul was only too well aware. We must not think that he went out to preach expecting God to bless his word merely because it was God's Word that he was preaching. Neither did he go out to preach expecting God to bless his word merely because God had so remarkably blessed him on previous occasions. Paul never presumed upon the power and blessing of God for his ministry. How do we know this? Towards the end of his second letter to the Thessalonians he asks the believers to pray for him. That request for prayer is itself significant. But what he asked them to pray concerning him is very important for us to notice: 'Finally, brothers, pray for us, that the word of the Lord may speed ahead and be honoured, *as happened among you*' (2 *Thess.* 3:1). In other words, the things that took place in Thessalonica when Paul first visited that city with the gospel (see *1 Thess.* 1), he wanted to see repeated time and again. Only God can make such things happen. Only he can make the gospel go forth 'in power, with the Holy Spirit and in full conviction'. Only the power of God can convert and transform sinners and fill them with the Spirit's joy, even in the midst of much affliction (*1 Thess.* 1:4–10).

'Pray for this, brothers', he says, in effect. 'I need God to bless my preaching, or else it will just be a matter of words. He must send down the Holy Spirit in power upon my preaching or else it will have no saving effect. Without him I can do nothing. But with him all things are possible!'

3

THE COMING OF THE SPIRIT

The Holy Spirit . . . had not yet fallen on any of them
(*Acts* 8:15–16).

Two interesting issues arise in the account of this great awakening in Samaria. The first relates to a topic concerned with biblical theology: how could the Samaritans believe in Jesus without initially being baptized with the Holy Spirit. The second relates to a topic that falls within the remit of pastoral theology: how should we understand the case of Simon the Magician, a man who appeared to be a Christian but who coveted the ability to control and dispense the power of God.

1. THE SAMARITAN BELIEVERS NOT AT FIRST BAPTIZED WITH THE HOLY SPIRIT

The words of our text have been referred to as 'perhaps the most extraordinary statement in Acts'. Here is a large group of people who received the word concerning the Lord Jesus and who believed in the Saviour. Upon profession of their faith they were baptized. Believing in Jesus Christ they were filled with great joy and yet, we are told that the Spirit was not given to them at the moment of their conversion. This is a strange occurrence because we

know from the Bible that it is the Spirit of God who re-
generates sinners and works faith and repentance in their
hearts. Personal faith and repentance and the reception
of the Spirit are always joined together in the Bible: 'Repent . . . and you will receive the gift of the Holy Spirit'
(*Acts* 2:38). How is it possible, then, for someone who is
'dead in trespasses and sins' to savingly confess Jesus
Christ as his Lord without the Holy Spirit? How could a
'natural man' whose heart is 'hostile to God' make such
a confession of Christ? Everything within the natural man
is dead to God. The Spirit must breathe the new life into
him. As Charles Wesley says:

> No man can truly say
> That Jesus is the Lord
> Unless Thou take the veil away,
> And breathe the living word;
> Then, only then, we feel
> Our interest in His blood,
> And cry with joy unspeakable:
> Thou art my Lord, my God.

Then how was it possible for these Samaritans to put
their trust in the blood of Christ without the Holy Spirit?
No one knows for sure the answer to that question;
the Bible does not give us an explanation of how the
saving work took place in the hearts of these Samaritan
believers.

We need to make it clear, however, that the Samaritans' condition was not the result of anything amiss in
Philip's ministry. He had preached as complete a gospel
as Peter had preached at Pentecost. Philip was a man 'full
of wisdom and of the Holy Spirit' while he proclaimed it.

The Samaritan believers were not like those in Ephesus who had not even heard that there was a Holy Spirit and whose baptism had been that of John the Baptist (*Acts* 19). The twelve men of Ephesus had not heard of the One who was to come after John, and so the life and works of the Lord Jesus had to be declared to them by Paul. The Samaritan believers, on the other hand, had listened to 'Philip as he preached good news about the kingdom of God and the name of Jesus Christ' (*Acts* 8:12). Therefore, neither the message nor the messenger were at fault.

Moreover, there was nothing lacking in the Samaritan's response to the gospel when they received the Word of God (*Acts* 8:14), nor in the close attention they paid to Philip (*Acts* 8:6), nor in their faith in what he had taught them (*Acts* 8:12), nor in the joy they knew as a result of the message they believed (*Acts* 8:8), nor in their baptism (*Acts* 8:12). All was admirable and exemplary, and yet there was a dimension of the person and work of the Holy Spirit that was absent from their lives.

As we think about the situation in Samaria we should keep in mind the case of the one hundred and twenty men whom Christ had gathered during his years of ministry. They could not be described as insincere or fake disciples. They had been baptized by Christ's apostles. They had accepted Christ's word and trusted in him. They had experienced great joy while listening to the Lord's preaching and teaching. Yet they were told to wait in Jerusalem until the Spirit came upon them.

It seems that a similar situation now existed in Samaria. The Lord sent Philip to the Samaritans and by his Spirit made an entrance for his Word among them. The Lord opened their hearts to believe the gospel and then filled those believing hearts with great joy. The Samaritans experienced the power of the Holy Spirit as Philip preached, counselled, prayed, and healed in their midst. Even so, the ascended Lord temporarily refrained from immediately pouring the Holy Spirit into these baptized believers. The Samaritans, just like the Lord's one hundred and twenty disciples, were to enter the orbit of redemption in two stages, and for a brief period of time they believed in Jesus without being baptized with the Holy Spirit.

Why did the Saviour work in this way with the Samaritans? The three thousand at Pentecost had repented and believed in the Lord Jesus Christ and were filled with the Spirit there and then. There was no two-step reception of the Spirit for them, or for the Ethiopian eunuch, the Philippian jailor, or Lydia. For them believing in Christ and the coming of the Spirit were concurrent.

The answer to this question lies in the fact that the gospel had crossed a significant border and had come to Samaria. Philip's ministry did not take place in Jerusalem, Bethlehem, Bethsaida or any other Jewish town for that matter, but in Samaria. These events happened in an Old Covenant community that had separated itself from the Jews and that lived on the north side of a partition that they had put up between themselves and Jerusalem, and behind which they did their own thing. These were people who had been in centuries-long rebellion against Jehovah, the God of Israel. Samaria was the spiritually compromised sector of the Holy Land. The Samaritans had had their own king, high priest, temple, and version of the Scriptures. They had rejected the kingly line of

Judah, the priestly line of Aaron, the city and temple of Jerusalem, and the Psalms and the Prophets of Holy Scripture. This had been the state of affairs within the Promised Land for a thousand years. Samaria was a rebellious nation that had long defied her Lord, and on account of this 'the Jews had no dealings with the Samaritans'.

Luke now tells us how a thousand years of division, exclusion, and contempt came to an end. We must remember that Luke's purpose in this book is not to give us a random sampling of early church piety and evangelistic activity. Acts 8 is not a brief but edifying episode from the 'good old days' when Christians were better than their modern counterparts. It is the history of how the Lord brought Samaria into the New Covenant blessing.

The church moved towards Samaria when it took its first steps beyond the borders of orthodox Judaism. The bridge to the Samaritans had to be crossed if the gospel was to be taken to the whole world. There could be no justification for enthusiastically taking the word into Europe, Africa, and Asia while withholding it from one's contemptible next-door neighbours. Samaria must hear the gospel of reconciliation and peace. Christ had commanded that it should be so. Religious and ethnic divisions, which spawned feuding generations, are to be overcome in Jesus Christ. This is what the gospel affirms and this is what must be practised. No human divisions can be allowed to spoil the unity the gospel establishes in Christ. This was a vitally important truth of which the young Jerusalem and Samaritan churches needed to be deeply persuaded.

At the outbreak of persecution in Jerusalem some of the believers there were scattered throughout Samaria

(*Acts* 8:1), and 'they went about preaching the word' (*Acts* 8:4). Among them was Philip who preached the gospel in a most powerful manner. Samaria received the gospel, trusted Christ, and was filled with joy. And yet 'the Holy Spirit . . . had not yet fallen on any of them' (*Acts* 8: 15–16).

As we continue to think about this strange and unusual circumstance, we should also note that the believers in Samaria were not given instructions about receiving the Spirit by any action on their part. For example, they were not told to follow a three-step formula in order to receive the Holy Spirit. Neither were they given a regimen of mortification, self-denial, and nights of prayer until a reluctant Lord relented and poured out the Spirit upon them. They were not urged to 'yield to the Spirit' or any such thing. They were certainly not coached to speak in tongues and so on. In fact, it seems that the Samaritans were not even informed that they did not have the Spirit! No, they were not told to do anything.

You see, the 'problem' was not theirs; the fault was not Philip's either. He did not need to attend a weekend conference on the theme 'Ministry that gives your church members the Holy Spirit'! When he later preached the gospel to the Ethiopian eunuch, Philip can send him on his way as a new convert who was already complete in Christ. Philip does not tell him to make an appointment with the apostles, Peter and John, before returning to his home in Africa. The very thought of the apostles moving around the whole eastern Mediterranean area, laying their hands on new groups of Christians so that they could receive the Spirit, is utterly ridiculous. When Paul asked the Galatians, 'Did you receive the Spirit by works of the law or by hearing with faith?' (*Gal.* 3:2), the answer he expected was that they had received the Holy Spirit through simply believing the gospel of Christ.

In other words, there was something uniquely differ-ent about Samaria and the Lord's delay in giving the Samaritans the Holy Spirit provided a significant and crucial lesson for the Jerusalem and Samaritan churches. Luke tells us that 'the apostles in Jerusalem heard that Samaria had accepted the word of God' (*Acts* 8:14). Immediately the Twelve sent Peter and John to Samaria. There is no one better equipped than they are to assess this 'surprising work of God'. They will make their observations as trustworthy witnesses and they will ascertain whether the Samaritans truly believe in the Saviour. If they can report to the church at Jerusalem that God is indeed welcoming the Samaritans into Christ's church, then there should be no quibbles about that fact. So off they go in an attempt to assure some sceptical members of the Jerusalem congregation (who may have been convinced that no good thing can come out of Samaria!) that the Samaritans have received the Holy Spirit just as they themselves had at Pentecost. They also give the right hand of fellowship to their new Samaritan brethren to show that they are reconciled to one another in Jesus Christ. Their visit will ensure that there will be no independent Samaritan denomination. They go there to gently convince them that the Samaritans have been wrong in their attitude to their southern Jewish brothers. It was the Lord's will that the Samaritans will receive his Spirit through his apostles from Jerusalem.

Now if you are still troubled as to how it is possible for the Samaritans to believe without being baptized with the Spirit – and who would not be – then there is no one at all who can tell you how it happened. The Bible does not analyse these events for us; it just tells us what happened and hints as to the reasons why it happened in this way.

But we need to be clear that the Samaritans received all the blessings of Christ's gospel through a simple trust in the Jesus Philip proclaimed to them. Peter and John did not come to Samaria with any extra information or a new set of instructions. There are no interrogations, no courses of study, and no weekends away from home to receive the Holy Spirit in a specially charged atmosphere. Very different were the apostles' methods: they came to Samaria, prayed for these Christians, simply laid their hands upon them and the Spirit was given to them (*Acts* 8:18).

One can imagine the scene: the entire Samaritan congregation gathered together and Philip welcoming Peter and John into their midst. Peter speaks, expressing his thankfulness and joy at seeing the kingdom of God extended into Samaria. The Saviour has indeed welcomed them into his church and Peter and John have been eyewitnesses of the grace of God among them. Yet the Lord has not sent his Holy Spirit upon them just yet. This is highly unusual, but the reason for this is the unique status of Samaria, the long standing rebellion, and the grief this has given to the God of Israel. But now through Jesus Christ full reconciliation has been accomplished for all Samaritans who believe on him. Christ's representatives have come so that the believing Samaritans might receive the Holy Spirit through their intercession.

Then the two apostles walk through the massed ranks of the congregation, one by one touching the believers on the arm or shoulder as they passed them by. The result was inexpressibly moving. Like lamps that are lit at a touch, so every member of that great congregation was given the Holy Spirit.

Did they speak in tongues? Luke does not tell us. He simply tells us that 'Simon saw the Spirit was given through the laying on of the apostles' hands' (*Acts* 8:18). Luke does not report that Simon heard them speaking in tongues. He saw something that connected the Spirit's coming with the action of Peter and John. But what it was we do not know, but tongues-speaking is not mentioned here. If Luke was convinced that speaking in tongues was the definitive proof that someone had been given the Holy Spirit, then it is strange for him not to mention it here. These people were believers, but they did not have the Holy Spirit. The apostles came and they received the Holy Spirit, but Luke does not say that this was known because they spoke in tongues. Here is an example of the Spirit falling upon people without any reference being made to the sign gifts of the Holy Spirit. Luke did not share the doctrine of Pentecostalists or Charismatics on this issue. Neither did the apostle Paul for his question, 'Do all speak in tongues?' clearly anticipated the answer, 'No' (*1 Cor.* 12:30).

Some of the greatest men in the history of the church have shared the same attitude as the apostle Paul on the issue of tongues-speaking. There was once a preacher in Australia who told a congregation that Dr Martyn Lloyd-Jones 'had spoken in tongues, though he would never admit it in public'. John Knight, who was troubled at this report, wrote to Dr Lloyd-Jones and asked him if this was true. In his reply the Doctor said, 'Many thanks for your kind letter. I am very happy to answer your question; and it is simply this, that I have never spoken in Tongues either in private or in public.'[1]

Perhaps they did speak in other languages in Samaria; we simply do not know. But where a text is silent, certainly about a matter as important as the marks of the Spirit's presence, then it is best for us to be silent too.

This peculiar feature of the great revival in Samaria is not teaching the separation of faith in the gospel of Christ from the receiving of the Holy Spirit, but rather their union. Luke significantly says in Acts 8:15–16, '. . . the Holy Spirit . . . had not yet fallen on any of them'. 'Not yet', says Luke, and by putting it in these terms he is strongly implying that the Spirit would inevitably fall on them simply because they had believed the gospel of Jesus. In other words, it is inconceivable that anyone who has received Christ's offer of salvation will not also be a Spirit-indwelt Christian.

What are we saying? Are we maintaining that every Christian gets everything there is to receive in regeneration and that what remains is a steady plod to heaven? Not at all! Such a message would be as unrealistic as a wedding sermon that informed the happy couple that since they have got each other now they have got all there is to get from their marriage. How mechanistic and unromantic! Every relationship is dynamic, mysterious, and growing, and none more so than that of the saint with his Saviour. There are fuller, richer times, and deeper, testing experiences in the Christian life. There are manifestations of Christ to the heart and also empowerings for service that we can only explain in terms of subsequent

[1] *D. Martyn Lloyd-Jones: Letters 1919–1981*, ed. Iain H. Murray (Edinburgh: Banner of Truth, 1994) p. 205.

fillings of the Spirit of Jesus. Hence, John Berridge sings,

> A single smile from Jesus given
> Will lift a drooping soul to heaven.

Have you ever experienced the Lord lifting up your downcast soul in this way?

However, the thing that we do not find in the book of Acts is a two-step reception of the blessings of salvation with each step depending on the obedient responses and efforts of man. Neither do we have the apostles (or their successors) today who can lay their hands on people and assure them that, on account of this touch, the Holy Spirit has been given to them.

I suppose I would rather go to the stake than allow a bishop to put his hands on my head and say to me, 'Receive the Holy Spirit'! Agreeing to that would mean denying my entire Christian experience and the conviction shaped by the Bible alone, that I, as a teenage boy sitting in a small Baptist chapel in the Rhymney Valley, heard the message of salvation and was indwelt by the Spirit when I entrusted myself to the Lord Jesus. How can I deny the faithful witness of the Spirit within me for over forty-five years by allowing another person to place his hands on my head and say such words?

The church no more needs Spirit-bestowing bishops than it needs priests and sacrifices of lambs, goats, and bulls! Any Pentecostal or Charismatic minister offering to do the same for me would be just as speedily rejected as the bishop! To receive all the blessings of salvation, including the forgiveness of sins and the Holy Spirit, we must go to God alone through the Lord Jesus Christ alone!

2. A SAMARITAN BELIEVER WANTS THE POWER TO GIVE THE SPIRIT.

'But there was a man named Simon, who had previously practised magic in the city and amazed the people of Samaria, saying that he was somebody great.' (*Acts* 8:9). These words introduce us to the fascinating character known as Simon Magus. *Magus* is the Greek word from which we get our word 'magic'. It means a magician, someone who manipulates preternatural forces for either the benefit or hurt of others. This sorcerer had dominated Samaria and was praised by the people as 'The Power of God that is called Great' (*Acts* 8:10). One wonders if some of the Samaritans even regarded him as an incarnation of deity?

Philip came to Samaria preaching Jesus Christ the incarnate Son of God and boasted of Jesus' cross and resurrection in Simon Magus' backyard, as it were. Once all the people gave their attention to Simon, but now they paid close attention to Philip. Once Simon had amazed them for a long time with his magic, but now it was Simon's turn to be amazed by the great signs and miracles he saw. Once Simon had boasted that he was someone great and people said of him 'This man is the power of God that is called Great', but now it is his turn to stand aside and bow the knee to Philip's all-conquering Saviour.

Simon claimed he had power to heal the sick, but we are told that the city was full of those who were possessed by evil spirits and that there were many who were paralysed and lame there whom Philip was able to heal (Acts 8:7). Simon's failure to do what he claimed he could do makes him the father of all such 'faith-healers'. There was little happiness in Samaritan homes until Philip came along with his gospel confirmed as it was with 'great signs and miracles' (*Acts* 8:13), and then 'there was much joy in that city' (*Acts* 8:8).

'Even Simon himself believed, and after being baptized he continued with Philip. And seeing signs and great miracles performed, he was amazed' (*Acts* 8:13). Outwardly, there seemed to be no difference between Simon and all the other new converts in Samaria. His profession of faith was indistinguishable from theirs. Knowing what Simon had been, the people would have watched him closely. What a great morale-boosting encouragement to Philip and the Samaritan believers to have a man like Simon among their number, attending all the church services, drinking in the Word, and enjoying the fellowship of saints.

When the apostles arrived, they prayed to the Lord that the Samaritans might receive the Spirit. Then, having placed their hands on them 'they received the Holy Spirit' (*Acts* 8:17).

Simon's response to this was not encouraging, to say the least. He did not recognize with a sad and heavy heart that Samaria had been out of step with God for a millennium, nor acknowledge the authority of Christ's apostles, nor rejoice in the newly established unity between old enemies in Christ. Rather he coveted the power he thought the apostles possessed and 'he offered them money saying, "Give me this power also, so that anyone on whom I lay my hands may receive the Holy Spirit"' (*Acts* 8:18–19). Certainly, on this occasion, God gave the Holy Spirit through the laying on of the apostles' hands. But it was wrong of Simon to think that the Spirit came because of that physical contact or that the Spirit was somehow given through the actual hands of the apostles. The Spirit came upon the Samaritans while the apostles touched them – yes, but he did not come through Peter and John's skin and pores. The Spirit came directly from the Father and the Son to the Samaritans, but he came only at the precise moment when the apostles placed their hands on them. The Lord placed this honour upon his servants for reasons we have already mentioned.

Simon, therefore, made the elementary mistake of thinking that the Spirit could be given because of some kind of controlling power that Peter and John possessed. But what followed was even worse. In coveting this power for himself, and willing to pay good money for it, Simon was thinking and acting like the old pagan professional he had been for so long. Did he want this power for his own selfish and greedy ends? Such motives must never lie within the heart of a Christian! Paul tells Timothy to beware of those who regard 'godliness as a means to financial gain' (1 Tim. 6:5, NIV).

This request of Simon for the ability to bestow the Spirit is a significant incident. Here is a professing Christian who desires the Holy Spirit so that he might have extraordinary spiritual power. What was the sorcerer's blunder? His biggest mistake was that he treated the Lord as an impersonal power rather than as an omnipotent person. David Feddes points out three errors that Simon made.[2]

First, notice that he *failed to appreciate the great difference between magic and miracles*. Magic is trying to harness unseen energies to achieve your own goals. A

[2] David Feddes, *The Radio Pulpit,* October 1996, p. 24.

miracle, on the other hand, occurs when a personal God answers the individual prayers of his people in a marvellous way to show his glory and goodness. Simon thought that Peter and John had some secret technique for controlling supernatural forces. But they had no such power in themselves; they prayed to God and depended entirely on how he chose to answer. The miracles and the coming of the Holy Spirit upon the people of Samaria was not the result of some technique they had mastered for harnessing and distributing a heavenly force.

Secondly, he *did not understand that the personal God cannot be bought as if he were some kind of 'thing'.* If God were an impersonal power, maybe this divine energy could be sold the way utility companies sell gas and electricity. But God is personal. He is not for sale, and it is a monstrous insult to try to pay for the Holy Spirit the way you would pay an electricity bill or the way you might pay for the rights to a patented bit of sorcery. God is not a saleable commodity.

Thirdly, Simon *did not grasp that the gospel of Jesus Christ cannot be blended with other spiritual and occult notions.* When the people of Samaria heard about Jesus, they did not combine their new faith in Jesus with their old faith in Simon. Rather, when they started believing in Jesus, they stopped believing in Simon. The two spiritualities just cannot be mixed. But Simon was still clearly attached to his past thoughts and practices.

He was a selfish single-minded man. He reckoned that the coming of the Holy Spirit gives people power, and that is why he wanted God – so that he could use God for himself. Simon wanted the Spirit in order to be able to give the Spirit to or withhold the Spirit from others. Such ability would give him, a mortal man, controlling power over men and women. He was not interested in getting to know the character of God or the person of Jesus Christ; he just wanted to tap into a new source of energy that would maximize his powers and give him a greater name than the one he had before. Simon was anxious to use divine power to expand his own potential and profits. He was passionate about himself, not about loving a personal Father in heaven.

To cry mightily to God for the Spirit so that we may serve the church better, become more Christlike, take up our cross each day and follow Christ, love our neighbour as ourselves, love our enemies, love God with all our heart, forgive and keep forgiving – is commendable and well pleasing to God. But it is wicked to ask for God's power to satisfy our own selfish, self-centred, and greedy ends.

When Simon offered money to have the Spirit, Peter was shocked by the notion that God's free gift could be bought by the highest bidder, as if the apostles could set a higher figure and cry, 'A thousand drachmas more and you can have the Spirit of God!' Rather Peter says, 'You thought you could obtain the gift of God with money!' (*Acts* 8:20). Simon Magus had apparently become a Christian by the free pardon of God received by faith in Jesus Christ – God's great free gift to the world. But he did not realize that the Christian life continues on the same basis as it started.

>'Tis mercy all, immense and free.

You do not have to bargain with God in order to obtain his gifts and graces. For every mile of the journey home, strength is freely given. For every new cross, thorn in the flesh, fiery trial, God supplies his free and all-sufficient grace.

Simon thought there was something he could do or pay to buy special favour from God. If he 'laid all on the altar' then he could procure this ability from above. Simon might well have given his imagination free rein as to what he could do with such power: he could 'blow' the Spirit upon people, or maybe 'wave' the Spirit on to them and down they would fall before him. Or he could dramatically cry, 'Receive him!', as he 'strutted his stuff' on the stage as the centre of everyone's attention.

Of course, God honours those who keep nothing back in his service. For example, there were those in the early church who placed the money from the sale of their lands and houses at the apostles' feet for the care of the poor (*Acts* 4:34). Barnabas is respected in Scripture for doing just that, but he did not do it in order to get more grace and favour from God (for then grace would cease to be grace). So why did he do it? He did it out of gratitude for the grace he had already freely received.

> Were the whole realm of nature mine,
> That were an offering far too small;
> Love so amazing, so divine,
> Demands my soul, my life, my all.

Simon thought he could buy this power of God and then tell his admirers that he had obtained it at great personal cost to himself.

Peter's words to Simon are among the most severe in the whole book of Acts, and even lengthier than his words of judgment on Ananias and Sapphira. These are harsh words but they are not sinful: 'May your silver perish

with you, because you thought you could obtain the gift
of God with money! You have neither part nor lot in this
matter, for your heart is not right before God. Repent,
therefore, of this wickedness of yours, and pray to the
Lord that, if possible, the intent of your heart may be
forgiven you. For I see that you are in the gall of bitterness and in the bond of iniquity' (*Acts* 8:20–23). Simon's
thinking is all wrong – 'You thought you could obtain
the gift of God with money'. Simon's 'heart is not right
before God'. Instead of being full of the Spirit, Simon
was 'in the gall of bitterness and in the bond of iniquity'.
Simon, did you really think that you were going to give
something to God, and because of that the Creator of the
universe, this ineffably sublime Lord God Almighty, would
give you something in return?

> Who has given a gift to him that he might be repaid? For
> from him and through him and to him are all things. To
> him be glory forever. Amen (*Rom.* 11:35–36).

Simon must repent and pray to the Lord. He must ask
God to forgive him. Simon, the great New-Age-like
magician, is at the end of the line. Was Peter saying to
Simon that he had never been a Christian, or that he had
taken too much baggage from his past into the kingdom
of God with him and it must be forsaken in repentance
and prayer? We do not know for sure, but we fear the
worst. And what of Simon's response, 'Pray for me to the
Lord, that nothing of what you have said may come upon
me' (*Acts* 8:24). We are glad to hear the once 'Great Power
of God' pleading with the apostles to pray for him. But
what are we to make of Simon's request? You solemnly
tell someone to repent of their sin and pray for forgive-

ness, and their response is, 'You pray for me.' Would you rejoice over such a reply? Where is the contrition? Where is the repentance? Simon was more concerned to escape God's judgment than to receive God's pardon. People who never darken the doors of a church often say to ministers, 'Pray for this and that.' Surely this was not a hopeful response. It reminds me of those who come forward to the platform in an evangelistic meeting and get someone to talk to them and pray over them, but their greatest need is to cry mightily to God for forgiveness, and not to cease crying until they are assured that God has heard them!

In the New Testament the coming of the Holy Spirit is a gift. He is freely given. His coming is all of God's grace and not because of our deserving. Our part is to receive the gift, never to purchase him with money or self-effort. Christ has purchased him for us. Our great High Priest freely pours out his Spirit upon us when we savingly believe his gospel. We do not buy him or work for him or merit him. The Holy Spirit is God's free gift to all who are bought at the price of the agony and blood of Jesus the Son of God.

3. THE REALITY OF THE SPIRIT'S PRESENCE

Let us return to the scene in Samaria and see how the Spirit came upon the believers there. Luke tells us that there was something to see and Simon was so struck by what he witnessed that he wanted the power to give the Holy Spirit and would have sacrificed much to obtain it. Let us think about the reality of the Spirit's power and presence that Simon witnessed for a moment. When religion is reduced to formal attendance at a church for an hour every week and when people go home no different from what they were when they came in – who would give a penny for the power behind that sort of thing? Who would sacrifice much for the light that comes from a match? Formal, neat, concise, precise, carefully ordered faith and worship is like a little religious frosting on a stale cake; it is worth nothing!

When this great awakening happened in Samaria lives were transformed and turned upside down. A whole new way of life began. People began to talk in a new and different way and they were full of enthusiasm about certain new things that had come into their lives. They had a new perspective on life, family, job, money, and possessions. They themselves were new people caught up by a new strength, and they were united in Christian fellowship by a glorious power that affected everything they did and thought.

I fear that many churchgoing people today are afraid of the implications of revival. They may have an outward form of godliness, but where is the power, the joy, the love, the transformed heart, and strong religious affections? They follow a rigidly prescribed Sunday pattern and are known as 'Christians'. But they take their Christianity in neat little capsules at certain set times and avoid overdosing at all costs! They like a 'beautiful' worship service with its formal order, routine, and decorum. But they seem to be insulated from the fire of the Spirit of God. They are unmoved by his life-giving power, and they never seem to get excited about Jesus Christ. They could never sincerely sing,

> All that thrills my soul is Jesus!
> He is more than life to me.

This is the way they want it. They may have a very fine doctrine of the Holy Spirit, and they may be very conservative in their beliefs, but they are just so staid, cold, and lifeless in their Christianity. There is nothing to see! They are afraid of those awakenings that are described for us in the Bible and in the pages of church history. Evangelical Christians in the Great Awakening of the eighteenth century were often called 'enthusiasts', but no one in their right mind could accuse their modern counterparts of enthusiasm!

Are you afraid of the Holy Spirit? Maybe you do not know the Lord Jesus Christ at all. Are you afraid of the Holy Spirit? Are you fearful that if you become a Christian and receive the Holy Spirit from God you will never be the same again? Yes, when the Holy Spirit comes upon a person there will be things in your life that other people will see and notice – I am not talking about irrational or stupid things but rather about transforming, elevating and life-enhancing changes.

My dear friend, do not be afraid of the Bible's teaching about revivals and spiritual awakenings. These are times when staggering advances are made for the kingdom of God. Many are brought into the kingdom of God, Christians are given a deep assurance of the truth of the gospel, the church increases in size and strength, and public wickedness is curtailed.

This is surely the need of the hour for the church in the Western world. Oh for times of refreshing to be sent from God upon us like those experienced in the past. Let me give you a little flavour of what those times of refreshing are like from the personal experience of Sarah Edwards.

She was the wife of Jonathan Edwards, the great New England preacher of the eighteenth century. On one occasion, when Jonathan Edwards was away from home, a certain Mr Buell was the visiting preacher. While he was leading in prayer, the words of Romans chapter 8 came powerfully to Sarah Edwards' mind and the force of their truth overwhelmed her. Later that evening when she was alone she recorded these words:

They appeared to me with undoubted certainty as the words of God, and as words which God did pronounce concerning me. I had no more doubt of it than I had of my being . . . and [I] had it strongly impressed on me, how impossible it was for anything in heaven or earth, in this world or the future, ever to separate me from the love of God which was in Christ Jesus. I cannot find language to express how certain this appeared – the everlasting mountains and hills were but shadows to it. My safety, and happiness, and eternal enjoyment of God's immutable love, seemed as durable and unchangeable as God himself. Melted and overcome by the sweetness of this assurance, I fell into a great flow of tears, and could not forbear weeping aloud. It appeared to me that God was my Father, and Christ my Lord and Saviour, that he was mine and I his . . . The presence of God was so near, and so real, that I seemed scarcely conscious of anything else . . . The peace and happiness which I hereupon felt, was altogether inexpressible. At the same time, I felt compassion and love for all mankind, and a deep abasement of soul, under a sense of my own unworthiness . . . I also felt myself more weaned from all things below, than ever before . . . My God was my all, my only portion.

This personal experience occurred during a time of an extraordinary work of God in America. About seven years earlier, in 1734–35, an awakening had taken place at Northampton, Massachusetts, and five years later a second, more extensive revival happened, which is now known as the Great Awakening. This work of God spread to many parts of the world. In Wales, Daniel Rowland and Howell Harris preached with great power and by God's grace transformed the Principality. In the same period Scotland witnessed a deepening spiritual concern and growing sense of unity among evangelical pastors. Whitefield and Wesley were also preaching to huge gatherings in the open-air throughout England.

When in 1740 Whitefield (aged twenty-five) arrived in North America he was invited to New England by several Boston ministers. This visit was to be 'like putting fire to tinder'. Whitefield preached to twenty thousand people in Boston and then travelled westward to Northampton. There he met Jonathan Edwards and Sarah his wife. Whitefield's preaching awakened the congregation. A second great revival began in Boston and Northampton in the autumn of 1740 that was more widespread in its extent than the work six years before. It prevailed for three years in more than one hundred and fifty congregations throughout New England and as far south as Virginia.

Sarah Edwards' experience of the divine love increased during the weeks that followed the initial experience we have referred to. She wrote:

Thursday night, Jan. 28, was the sweetest night I ever had in my life. I never before, for so long a time together, enjoyed so much of the light, and rest, and sweetness of heaven in my soul . . . All night I continued in a constant, clear, and lively sense of the heavenly sweetness of Christ's excellent and transcendent love, of his nearness to me, and of my dearness to him; with an inexpressibly sweet calmness of soul and an entire rest in him. I seemed to myself to perceive a glow of divine love come down from the heart of Christ in heaven, into my heart, in a constant stream, like a stream . . . of sweet light. At the same time, my heart and soul all flowed out in love to Christ; so that there seemed to be a constant flowing and reflowing of heavenly and divine love, from Christ's heart to mine . . .

This lively sense of the beauty and excellency of divine things continued during the morning, accompanied with peculiar sweetness and delight . . . The spiritual beauty of the Father and the Saviour seemed to engross my whole mind . . . I never felt such an emptiness of self-love, or any regard to any private, selfish interest of my own . . . The glory of God seemed to be all, and in all, and to swallow up every . . . desire of my heart.

I felt at the same time an exceedingly strong and tender affection for the children of God, and realized, in a manner exceedingly sweet and ravishing, the meaning of Christ's prayer in John 17:21, 'That they all may be one, as thou Father art in me, and I in thee, that they also may be one in us.' This union appeared to me an inconceivable, excellent and sweet oneness; and at the same time I felt that oneness in my soul, with the children of God who were present . . . So conscious was I of the joyful presence of the Holy Spirit, I could scarcely refrain from leaping with transports of joy . . . My soul was filled and overwhelmed with light, and love, and joy in the Holy Ghost.

I wished to have the world join me in praising him . . .
I felt a love to all mankind far beyond all that I had ever
felt before. I thought, if I were surrounded by enemies,
who were venting their malice and cruelty upon me, in
tormenting me, it would still be impossible that I should
cherish any feelings towards them but those of love, and
pity, and ardent desires for their happiness.

Her experience was never an excuse to look down on
other Christians or judge them. 'To do this', she said,
'seemed abhorrent to every feeling of my heart.' She also
sensed, in a powerful way, that a great part of true Christianity lay not just in personal experiences but in duties
and responsibilities to others.

Sarah Edwards then felt with renewed force the
majesty of God. 'Towards night' she said, 'I had a deep
sense of the awful greatness of God . . . It seemed to me
that we ought greatly to revere the presence of God, and
to behave ourselves with the utmost solemnity and
humility . . . In the evening, these words, in the *Peniten-
tial Cries* – "The Comforter is come!" – were accompanied
to my soul with such conscious certainty, and such
intense joy, that immediately it took away my strength,
and I was falling to the floor, when some of those who
were near me caught me and held me up. And when I
repeated the words to the bystanders, the strength of my
feelings was increased. The name – "The Comforter" –
seemed to denote that the Holy Spirit was the only and
infinite Fountain of comfort and joy . . . These words
"The Comforter" seemed . . . enough to fill heaven and
earth.'

Her husband welcomed Sarah's immediate experience
of God. Though one of the greatest intellects America ever

produced, he did not think his wife was becoming a religious fanatic. If her brain was becoming confused, he wrote, 'let my brain be evermore possessed of that happy distemper'. He added, 'I pray God that the world of mankind be all seized with' the same experience. We ought to remember that Jonathan and Sarah had a family of eleven children, and Sarah Edwards was a polite, practical nononsense woman, who did not spend her whole time in reading the Bible but entered into all her household work with determination and joy. When her husband died tragically two months after taking up his new position as the President of the College of New Jersey (later to become Princeton University), Sarah bowed in humility before God's will, comforting and strengthening the faith of her children.

David Feddes makes some helpful comments on the experience of the Holy Spirit in a true revival. He says,

> What the Holy Spirit did in Sarah Edwards is in keeping with what the Bible says about the Spirit. Scripture says that the Spirit moves us to call God our Father. 'The Spirit himself testifies with our spirit that we are God's children' (*Rom.* 8:16). The Spirit who inspired the writing of the Bible applies and seals the Bible's words on the heart, as Sarah Edwards experienced. The Spirit does not give experience for the sake of experience, but always draws the mind and heart to Jesus Christ and to God the Father, as the Bible says (*John* 16:13–15), and as Sarah testified. The Holy Spirit convinces people of their own sin and of God's forgiveness, and in his own time and his own way, the Spirit may also seal their hearts with a powerful immediate assurance of God's favour beyond anything they've tasted before.

The apostle Paul prays that his readers may 'grasp how wide and long and high and deep is the love of Christ and to know this love that surpasses knowledge – that you may be filled to the measure of all the fullness of God' (*Eph.* 3:18–19). Paul also speaks of 'the peace of God, which transcends all understanding' (*Phil.* 4:7), and Peter tells of 'an inexpressible and glorious joy' (*1 Pet.* 1:3). Such delight in God made Sarah willing to give up anything else, just as it moved Paul to say, 'I consider everything a loss compared to the surpassing greatness of knowing Christ Jesus' (*Phil.* 3:8).

Satisfaction in God moves the soul to passionate love for the Lord and also for others. The Spirit gives a taste of heaven that transforms your life and behaviour on earth. 'The fruit of the Spirit is love, joy, peace, patience, kindness, goodness, faithfulness, gentleness and self-control' (*Gal.* 5:22–23).

Some people of less maturity than Sarah Edwards have been tempted to make their own marvellous experiences an excuse to look down on others, and that sometimes makes people resent any talk about such intense and glorious blessings from the Spirit. But our response to the Spirit's touch should be love and humility, not pride.

Another mistake in speaking of the Spirit's ministry is to insist that only the act of speaking in tongues is the sure mark of the Spirit's richest blessing in a person's life. The Bible doesn't say that an outpouring of the Holy Spirit always produces the gift of tongues. Sarah Edwards didn't speak in tongues, and neither did most other people in the Great Awakening, and yet the mighty outpouring of the Spirit upon them was undeniably real.

Others have placed great emphasis on physical effects such as leaping for joy or fainting from an overwhelming sense of God's majesty. This, too, can become an obstacle if it is implied that being filled with the Spirit is synonymous with fainting or jumping up and down. Here, too, we can learn from Sarah Edwards. Although the Spirit's outpouring sometimes had an impact on her body, she always considered such things as mere side-effects, not something to be focused on. Her focus was on Christ, and that's where she wanted others to focus as well.

When you think about the Spirit's outpouring and its effect on believers, don't be so afraid of excesses or oddities or errors that you quench the Spirit himself. Instead, keep seeking more and more of the Spirit's blessing in your life. Don't just seek an experience – seek God. The intensity of experience may vary from person to person as it pleases God to give his blessing, but the outpouring of the Holy Spirit is real, and we should be seeking that reality more and more.

So pray earnestly that you may know Christ more fully and directly through the touch of his Spirit, and pray that the Holy Spirit's mighty power of renewal and revival may flood many others in your community and throughout the world.

As the apostle Paul put it, 'I keep asking that the God of our Lord Jesus Christ, the glorious Father, may give you the Spirit of wisdom and revelation, so that you may know him better. I pray also that the eyes of your heart may be enlightened in order that you may know the hope to which he has called you, the riches of his glorious inheritance in the saints, and his incomparably great power for us who believe' (*Eph.* 1:17–19).

4

ONE MAN AS IMPORTANT
AS A CITY OF MEN

Now an angel of the Lord said to Philip, 'Rise and go
towards the south to the road that goes down from
Jerusalem to Gaza.' This is a desert place. And he
rose and went. And there was an Ethiopian . . .
(*Acts* 8:26–27).

We have looked at this great awakening in Samaria,
which began with Philip's preaching of the gospel
and which resulted in many conversions among the
Samaritan people. Under the gracious and powerful
influences of the Holy Spirit, the people of Samaria had
given Philip their attention, marvelled at the miracles he
wrought, believed his message, professed their faith in
Christ through baptism, and experienced great joy.

One could be forgiven for thinking that Philip had his
true vocation in life – the Evangelist and Church-Planter
of Samaria. Surely his remaining years would be spent in
organizing and instructing the churches of Samaria and
publishing the good news of Jesus the Messiah throughout this neglected and dark corner of Palestine? As Peter
and John departed Samaria for Jerusalem they may well

have encouraged Philip by saying: 'Philip, the Lord has opened to you a great and effectual door for gospel work. Be steadfast, immovable, always abounding in the work of the Lord. See that you fulfil the ministry that you have received in the Lord.' It seems likely that they would have encouraged him to carry on the glorious work in the same way as he had so promisingly begun.

1. PHILIP WAS SENT FROM THE MANY TO THE ONE

But suddenly, Philip abandons his new converts. He had come to Samaria at the outbreak of persecution in Jerusalem. We are not told that Philip had been set apart by the church as their missionary to the Samaritans. It seems more likely that he came to Samaria on his own initiative, acting in accordance with the Lord's words that the Samaritans were not to be neglected in the work of missions. If that was the case and he had come to Samaria on his own initiative, it is interesting to note that he did not leave on his own initiative: no, he only left this scene of very fruitful labour at the express intervention and command of God.

When the angels gathered together in heaven that day to receive their instructions from the Lord God, one of them was given this command: 'Go to Samaria and tell Philip to leave the city and to take the road south that goes from Jerusalem to Gaza through the desert' (*Acts* 8:26). That is exactly what the angel did, and we are told that Philip 'rose and went' (*Acts* 8:27). He left a scene of unparalleled blessing and opportunity, a place where he was revered by a whole congregation, and went immediately to do as the Lord directed.

In this act of obedience to the Lord's call Philip showed himself to be a true child of Abraham. When the Lord appeared to Abram in Ur of the Chaldeans and told him to 'Go from your country and your kindred and your father's house to the land that I will show you' (*Gen.* 12:1), 'Abram went, as the LORD had told him' (*Gen.*12:4). With the same obedient faith Philip 'rose and went'. The Christian lives by faith, trusting God. In all areas of life the Lord's Word is to be received by faith, lovingly cherished in the heart and cheerfully obeyed in the life. When the Lord's Word says, 'Stop', the Christian stops. When his Word says, 'Do this', the Christian does it. 'Trust and obey' are the happy Christian's watchwords. Upon the principle of 'faith working through love' (*Gal.* 5:6) the Christian life begins and continues till the end.

When Philip began serving the Lord there were clear indications in his life that he had learned this lesson. Now, once again, he obeys the Lord's command and he sets out on his sixty-mile walk towards Gaza. One can imagine the kind of thoughts that must have been coursing through Philip's mind during this lonely walk. Did he think about all the way his Saviour had led him so far? It was not that long ago that he was just an 'anonymous' church member of the Jerusalem congregation. Then the church appointed him as one of their deacons to relieve Peter and the other apostles of the responsibilities associated with the ministry of mercy to the church's dependent widows. Moreover, indelibly marked on his memory was the terrible but glorious day when his dear friend, brother, and fellow deacon Stephen was stoned to death for preaching Jesus Christ to the Jews. Philip's mind may also have been filled with the fresh memories of what the Lord had just recently accomplished through his own preaching of the gospel in the land of Samaria – the mighty signs and wonders, and the conversion and transformation of so many men and women, and the filling of the city with joy. The Lord had done so much through him, and all in such a relatively short period of time. But all that was now in the past. He was alone now, just walking through the desert.

How mysterious are the ways of God! How strange are some of God's dealings with us! Philip had two days in which to reflect on all that had happened in his life. Perhaps he sang the praises of God as he walked the desert road. Perhaps he also was puzzled as to why the Lord had called him away from the revival in Samaria and perplexed as to what the Lord would have him do in the barren desert. Then, suddenly, he saw a little party of African travellers in the distance. As he lengthened his stride with a sense of anticipation, the Spirit said to him, 'Go over and join this chariot.' Without any hesitation, 'Philip ran' over to it (*Acts* 8:30).

Philip's actions reveal the true spirit of an evangelist. He is always ready to give a reason for the hope that is within him, always abounding in the work of the Lord, prepared to speak a word for Jesus in season and out of season. Indeed, in the aftermath of Stephen's martyrdom it had only taken a sense of personal conviction for Philip to go to Samaria and preach the gospel to the people there. Following the directions of an angel from heaven and the Holy Spirit, Philip left Samaria for the desert road to Gaza where he was to meet the Ethiopian in his chariot. To leave a thriving congregation for a desert road required a deep assurance that such a step was what God wanted him to do. It was still the 'honeymoon' period for pastor and people in Samaria: Philip was deeply loved by his flock who were filled with joy because of the wonderful message he had brought them. How could he leave the thronged streets of the city for the empty desert road, the fellowship of the saints for a lonely wilderness, an enormous crowd for a solitary individual, fame for anonymity? One wonders whether Philip questioned the divine command when it came?

Did he think to himself that he ought to use his common sense, and ask why he should go to the empty desert when God was clearly using him to establish churches in densely populated Samaria? Did he say, 'Lord, why the desert? I was thinking more in terms of a move to the great cities of Athens and Rome.' Perhaps he thought that the angel had made a mistake and brought the right message but to the wrong person!

If Philip was a man like us, he probably did face some form of temptation that sought to divert him from obeying the Lord's will. However, the Lord made his will clear, not only by employing the angelic messenger but also by speaking to Philip directly. I do not know what it is like to hear the voice of the Holy Spirit as Philip heard it. When the Jews heard God the Father speaking to Jesus they thought it sounded like thunder (*John* 12:29), and the voice of the Spirit may have thundered similarly to Philip. The Spirit's voice was certainly distinctive and personal. The Scripture here does not tell us that Philip had 'strong feelings' and 'felt led' to approach the Ethiopian's chariot. No, the Holy Spirit is a person and, as a person, he spoke these words to Philip, 'Go to that chariot and stay near it.'

William Chalmers Burns left a spiritual awakening in Dundee, where many professed faith under his ministry, to go to China as a gospel missionary. To turn one's back on a great harvest of souls in order to plough up a hard and barren land one needs to be firmly persuaded of the will of God. But an angel did not speak to him, nor did he hear the voice of the Holy Spirit, but he had the deepest assurance, drawn from the Word of God, that this was indeed God's will for him. He needed nothing more than this to convince him of his calling to take the gospel to China. However, the years in China saw only a small number of converts gathered into the kingdom of God. Had William Chalmers Burns mistaken his calling? Had he wasted his time? Was he 'out of the will of God'? No, far from it! Burns' labours laid a foundation for future missionary work in China. In later years, Hudson Taylor built on the pioneering work Burns had done.

Philip's unexpected departure from Samaria was ordained of God so that the gospel would come to a solitary Ethiopian. But what would the consequences be of Philip's testimony to the Ethiopian eunuch? What would the conversion of this man mean for Africa? Think of it: before a single European had been converted to Christ, this African, an important official in charge of all the treasury of Candace, queen of the Ethiopians, was to hear about the Saviour and trust in Christ and take the glorious gospel home to that great continent.

2. PHILIP WAS SENT TO AN OUTSIDER

The Ethiopian eunuch was an unusual individual. Luke does not tell us his name. It seems that he had made a long pilgrimage from his homeland to Jerusalem and that while in the city he had obtained a copy of the scroll of Isaiah's prophecy. He was a highly intelligent man and deeply religious. He held a very important office in the government of Ethiopia, but in spite of all these privileges and blessings he was an outsider as far as the Old Covenant was concerned. The Ethiopian was a Gentile and he was also a eunuch. Deuteronomy 23:1 explicitly stated that 'No one whose testicles are crushed or whose male organ is cut off shall enter the assembly of the Lord.' Though this man was 'a God-fearer' who confessed Yahweh, the God of Israel as the only God, he was denied the status of a convert to Judaism, and was excluded from the Court of Israel in the Temple.

Jesus had come 'to seek and to save that which was lost' and it was to reach such a lost outsider that the Lord sent Philip on this strange errand to the lonely desert road. Certain prophecies relating to the new Messianic age were now about to be fulfilled. If we could have asked an expectant Jewish believer what the Old Testament prophesied about the New Covenant age, he would have said that the Gentiles were going to be converted to the Lord. He might have quoted from Psalm 68:31: 'Nobles shall come from Egypt; Cush [the upper Nile region] shall hasten to stretch out her hands to God.' He might also have turned to Psalm 87:3–4: 'Glorious things of you are spoken, O city of God. Among those who know me I mention Rahab and Babylon; behold, Philistia and Tyre, with Cush – "This one was born there", they say.' Another relevant passage is Isaiah 11:10–11: 'In that day the Root of Jesse, who shall stand as a signal for the peoples – of him shall the nations enquire, and his resting-place shall be glorious. In that day the Lord will extend his hand yet a second time to recover the remnant that remains of his people from Assyria, from Egypt, from Pathros, from Cush, from Elam, from Shinar, from Hamath, and from the coastlands of the sea.'

Jewish believers who truly understood the Old Testament Scriptures would have been familiar with these Messianic promises and soon their God-fearing Gentile neighbours would also grasp their truth. The promised Christ had come and the Lord's kingdom was spreading throughout the world.

This was that of which the prophets spoke. Africa would send both tribute and worshippers to Jerusalem. What he was seeing seemed to say to Philip: 'See this Ethiopian coming to Jerusalem, and now returning home? This is the fulfilment of that Messianic prophecy, Philip!' What Isaiah could only predict and look forward to in anticipation, Philip and the apostles were privileged to see.

Besides being a Gentile, this man was excluded from the Old Covenant community and could not participate in the fellowship of the people of God on account of his being a eunuch; this, too, was all about to change. The Scriptures had also foretold the blessing that eunuchs would be given in the last days:

> Let not the foreigner who has joined himself to the LORD say, 'The LORD will surely separate me from his people'; and let not the eunuch say, 'Behold, I am a dry tree.' For thus says the LORD: 'To the eunuchs who keep my Sabbaths, who choose the things that please me and hold fast my covenant, I will give in my house and within my walls a monument and a name better than sons and daughters; I will give them an everlasting name that shall not be cut

off. And the foreigners who join themselves to the LORD, to minister to him, to love the name of the LORD, and to be his servants, everyone who keeps the Sabbath and does not profane it, and holds fast my covenant – these I will bring to my holy mountain, and make them joyful in my house of prayer . . . for my house shall be called a house of prayer for all nations' (*Isa.* 56:3–7).

What Isaiah had prophesied in days of old is now taking place before Philip's very eyes. The evangelist knew that Joel's prophecy had been fulfilled recently at Pentecost. He had also witnessed wonderful things taking place in despised Samaria, and now it is the turn of this Gentile eunuch to be brought into the blessedness of this bright new gospel age. These things said to him, 'Philip, this is what was uttered by the prophets!' Satan is to deceive the nations of the world no longer. The kingdom of God is breaking forth out of its narrow little piece of land on the eastern coast of the Mediterranean. The apostle John grasped this truth when he wrote: 'Christ is the propitiation for our sins, and not for ours only but also for the sins of the *whole world*' (*1 John* 2:2).

The regulations in the law of Moses that excluded uncircumcised Gentiles and eunuchs from the fellowship of the Lord's people were tied to a sanctuary of stone in the city of Jerusalem that was soon to be demolished. It would not be long before God would teach Peter that the ancient distinctions between clean and unclean foods – and clean and unclean people – had served its purpose and was now a thing of the past.

The message of the kingdom of God was no longer to be contained within the boundaries of this little nation. It was going to spread like wildfire from Jerusalem, throughout all Judea and Samaria, and to the uttermost ends of the earth. The kingdom of God was not to be understood in terms of diet, circumcision, race, annual religious feasts, or a holy city. No, it was about righteousness, peace and joy in the Holy Spirit. After Pentecost none of those former things was the sign that men were holy, or were accepted by God.

All those former things belonged to the outward administration of the Old Covenant. From the day of Pentecost forward God accepted men from all nations whose hearts were sanctified by faith in his only begotten Son, Jesus Christ. Jesus Christ is the only way to God for all kinds of people everywhere.

'What God has made clean, do not call common', Peter was told by a voice from heaven (*Acts* 10:15). The apostle had to grasp the implications of these words. Later, addressing Cornelius the Gentile centurion, he said, 'God has shown me that I should not call any man common or unclean' (*Acts* 10:28). In other words, there are no 'second-class' citizens in the kingdom of God. Within Christ's church there is no discrimination against Greek or Barbarian, bond or freeman, eunuch or father, man or woman, Jew or Gentile.

None of these criteria can be applied to bar any from believing the gospel and finding acceptance with God through Christ. None is barred. Christ has opened the door of salvation to all who will enter on his terms. To all kinds of men and women the free offer of Christ the Saviour is made.

Now then, where was the house of prayer for all nations to be found? It was no longer to be found in that stone temple in Jerusalem, which the monstrous Herod had constructed. The temple had served its purpose. When Jesus cried 'It is finished', and then died, the veil in the temple was torn in two from top to bottom. The earthly temple's usefulness was finished and soon it would be razed to the ground, never to be constructed again. The God of the temple has come amongst us in a new and better way in his incarnate Son, Jesus Christ. This is why we can sing:

> Jesus, where'er Thy people meet,
> There they behold Thy mercy-seat;
> Where'er they seek Thee Thou art found,
> And every place is hallowed ground.
>
> For Thou, within no walls confined,
> Inhabitest the humble mind;
> Such ever bring Thee where they come,
> And going take Thee to their home.

Jesus taught a Samaritan woman this very truth when he said to her:

> Woman, believe me, the hour is coming, when neither on this mountain nor in Jerusalem will you worship the Father . . . But the hour is coming, and is now here, when the true worshippers will worship the Father in spirit and truth, for the Father is seeking such people to worship him. God is spirit, and those who worship him must worship in spirit and truth' (*John* 4:21-24).

The place of worship and prayer can now be found anywhere, even by the side of a desert road on the way south to Gaza. And it was just here that a castrated Ethiopian found the Saviour and was cleansed from sin to serve the living God.

3. PHILIP ASKED THE EUNUCH THE RIGHT QUESTION

When Philip got alongside the chariot he heard the man from Africa reading aloud from the writings of Isaiah. Reading while travelling is a most popular pastime for many people. Sometimes when travelling by air I walk to the back of the cabin and glance down the aisles to see what books my fellow passengers are reading. If they are reading a Bible I take that as an invitation to stop and introduce myself, and ask a little about them and how it is that they are reading Scripture. My heart has been stirred sometimes when I see other familiar books being read, and I take my courage in my hands and stop and say, 'Are you enjoying that book. I have read it and enjoyed it.' I have had some unexpected conversations about books while on my travels.

'Do you understand what you are reading?' Philip asked (*Acts* 8:30). The eunuch said to him, 'How can I, unless someone guides me?' The words of Isaiah are generally lucid. They are simple enough for almost anyone to understand their basic meaning. That is not to say that all parts of Isaiah, or the Bible for that matter, are equally clear, or that there are no difficult sections to grapple with. The apostle Peter writes about Paul's letters and comments, 'There are some things in them that are hard to understand' (2 *Pet.* 3:16). There is probably no biblical writer about whom such words could not apply. But, as Martin Luther affirmed, what is obscure in one part of Scripture is stated more clearly elsewhere. You do not have to be a genius or an expert to understand the Bible, but you do have to read it carefully, think about what you have read, and respond in faith to the truth that it teaches. As Psalm 119:130 puts it, 'The unfolding of your words gives light; it imparts understanding to the simple.'

Sadly, there have been times in history when the religious elite discouraged ordinary people from reading the Bible. They claimed that a person had to be well educated to know what the Bible was saying. But the Word of God does not speak only to scholars; it was not written just for their benefit. The Scriptures are for ordinary people and for all people. God speaks through laws and stories and poems and letters that can be grasped by ordinary people. The Bible 'gives understanding to the simple'. Biblical Christianity is not an esoteric religion, the understanding of which only comes when you skilfully crack a 'Bible-code' that reveals Scripture's real but hidden message.

What sort of God would reveal his love and salvation in language so abstract, and concepts so profound, that only someone who belonged to the intelligentsia could understand them? Jesus came preaching the kingdom of God and gathered a congregation of very ordinary people around his pulpit. The common people heard him gladly (*Mark* 12:37, AV). On the day of Pentecost the word preached by Peter was plain enough to the three thousand who repented and believed it, and they all continued to gather round the 'pulpit' of the apostles' doctrine. The Word of God creates, sanctifies and strengthens the church. The Bible is the best book to help us understand the Bible. In God's light we see light.

Even children may understand the Bible. Certain parts of Scripture are addressed specifically to them. For example, the book of Proverbs addresses children directly in many places. In Ephesians Paul speaks to the children in the church at Ephesus and give them this command: 'Children, obey your parents in the Lord, for this is right' (*Eph.* 6:1). Mary Jones was a just a young person who lived in Wales two centuries ago. Though only a young girl, she longed to have a Bible of her own, and there were many other young people with the same longing as Mary Jones!

The writer and bookseller William Hone had been raised in a Christian home but had turned against the Christian faith. In fact, in 1817 he was prosecuted for a parody of a Christian creed. One day as he was riding through Wales he came across a girl sitting in the sunshine on her front doorstep reading the Bible. 'Doing your task?' he called out to her. She did not understand his meaning at first. 'You have been set the task of reading the Bible?', he asked her in more deliberate tones. 'Oh no', she protested, 'I only wish I could read it all day long!' Her sincere love for the Word of God touched him as nothing else had done. As Job said, 'God maketh my heart soft' (*Job* 23:16, AV), and the words of that little girl, expressing as they did her love for her Bible, were the means of softening William Hone's hard heart. After he had turned to God in repentance and professed the faith he had for so long rejected, he wrote some fine verses, acknowledging:

> The proudest heart that ever beat
> Has been subdued in me:
> The wildest will that ever rose
> To scorn Thy cause or aid Thy foes
> Is quelled, my God, by Thee.

So, in the Scriptures God speaks to men in a way that can be understood by the simplest of men and women, boys and girls. God speaks to us by his living Word. Once, when Thomas Boston was reading Psalm 121 at family worship, the thought came to him that those very words were written just for him as if there were no one else in the whole world to which they could apply. Unbelieving men sometimes try to keep a gospel minister at arms' length and hide their unbelief behind the smoke screen of an honest agnosticism by claiming that they are 'seeking after truth'. In prayer to God his Father, the Lord Jesus Christ said, 'Your word is truth' (*John* 17:17). If the agnostic wants to find what he is seeking for then he must come to the Bible and sit under the best Bible teaching ministry available to him. By the Scriptures God speaks, and his words are truth and life. God has also given pastor-teachers to his church who expound the Scriptures and apply them to the hearts and lives of the people. Through their faithful preaching and teaching God saves sinners and strengthens saints.

God sent Philip to the Ethiopian eunuch and down through the centuries he has sent many a Christian to meet those whose hearts are empty and who long to know more of the Word of God. The eunuch was grappling with the meaning of a particular portion of Isaiah's prophecy. He struggled to understand it because he could not figure out about whom the prophet was writing. Was he writing about himself? Surely not! He must then have been writing about someone else, but whom? Isaiah doesn't tell us. Who is it? Who fits this description? The Ethiopian did not know of whom Isaiah was speaking because he had not heard about Jesus of Nazareth. He only had the Old Testament Scriptures, but now Philip was to become his New Testament!

'Do you understand what you are reading?', he asked. When we invite strangers to come to church with us we should ask them after the service if they understood the sermon, and if they have not we should enquire further into what it was they did not understand. This is something we can also profitably do with our children.

4. PHILIP UNDERSTOOD THE SCRIPTURES AND EXPLAINED THEM TO HIM

'Then Philip opened his mouth, and beginning with this Scripture he told him the good news about Jesus' (*Acts* 8:35). Philip's own wonderful personal experience was not the subject of his conversation with the Ethiopian. Neither did he speak to him about all the amazing miracles God enabled him to do in Samaria. While Philip is portrayed to us as a youthful and energetic evangelist, the thing that Luke seems to be most anxious for us to notice here is the way Philip used the Scriptures to communicate the message of the gospel to this needy man.

Picture the scene: the Ethiopian has the Word of God, and is reading it, but he cannot identify the One about whom it speaks. He needs a guide, an interpreter, an expositor of the word. Who is going to explain it to him? He needs someone who himself has a good grasp of the message of the Bible.

In 1955 two boys in my year at school professed faith in Jesus Christ and their conversions set the senior classes buzzing with keen discussion about religion. One of the boys who benefited most from this discussion was a Jehovah's Witness who had been drilled in memorizing and understanding the Watchtower version of the Bible. I remember feeling very inadequate in answering his questions at that time. In fact, I felt that I could not answer him, not because there were no answers to such questions, but because my own knowledge of the Bible was so poor. I hardly knew the Bible and most of the other boys were in deeper darkness than myself. Looking back, I have to say that very few of those teenagers went to church in those 'good old days'; perhaps only two or three others from my class attended church regularly. It was not long before I saw my own ignorance of Scripture as a hindrance in being a good witness to the Lord Jesus Christ among the lost boys of south Wales.

Ioan Thomas listened intently as Howell Harris preached the Word of God with great power on one occasion. In the sermon he said to his congregation, 'You have turned the pages of the Bible often for forty years, and yet you don't know more of God than a dog knows.' Ioan Thomas thought to himself, 'That's me!' Well, at the tender age of sixteen, I knew exactly how Ioan Thomas felt, for I, too, knew very little of the Bible. The only thing I could do to remedy the situation was to begin reading the Bible every evening, and as I read it my understanding of the Bible began to grow. I can remember the first time I read Paul's letters to the Thessalonians, and thinking to myself, 'Right! This is where the New Testament teaches us that Jesus is coming again.' Now that was a tiny but significant step forward for me. I was on the Christian learning curve and it was rising fast!

As we bear our witness to the Lord in the world we ourselves grow in the grace and knowledge of the Lord Jesus Christ. Jay Adams tells the story of something that happened to a member of his congregation the day after he had preached a sermon on the deity of Christ. The Christian woman phoned him and in a whispering voice asked, 'Where in Scripture do we find that Jesus Christ is God?'

'Why are you whispering?' Adams enquired.

'I've got a Jehovah's Witness in the kitchen with me and he's winning the argument.'

'But last night in church I gave many verses from the New Testament to show that the Saviour is divine, and you were present.'

'Yes, I know,' she said, 'but I didn't know I needed that then.' It was when she came to the front line of Christian service and had to think through her faith and put her beliefs into words that she saw the importance of understanding what the Bible teaches.

Christian service and particularly personal evangelism provide us with strong incentives to read and get to grips with the message of the Bible. The questions we face and the discussions we hold with our unbelieving friends and neighbours make us want to get back to the study, open up our Bibles again, and search their pages with renewed zeal. We long to be better equipped to speak of

> The glories of our God and King,
> The triumphs of His grace!

It is when we have to explain what we believe that we realize there is nothing God delights to bless and use so much as his own precious Word. In Isaiah 55:10–11 God spoke about his Word in these terms:

For as the rain and snow come down from heaven and do not return there but water the earth, making it bring forth and sprout, giving seed to the sower and bread to the eater, so shall my word be that goes out from my mouth; it shall not return to me empty, but it shall accomplish that which I purpose, and shall succeed in the thing for which I sent it (*Isa.* 55:10–11).

The Word of God is like rainfall on land that has been parched by drought; it waters and revives it and enables it to bring forth fruit. The Protestant Reformation of the sixteenth century is a wonderful example of the powerful impact of the Word of God; at that time the Bible transformed a whole continent. Nothing is so divinely effective as Scripture. 'It shall not return to me empty', God says.

God's Word is like the rain. It falls wherever it pleases, sometimes like a fine drizzle, sometimes like tempestuous torrents. We cannot clap our hands and say, 'No rain today', or 'Plenty of showers this week'. It falls at God's will and it accomplishes the purpose for which he sends it. In spiritual terms, Samaria was a land without heavenly rain for centuries, but then Philip came to Samaria with the Word of God, and God opened the heavens and down poured the showers of blessing (*Ezek.* 34:26). Likewise, God had determined to save an Ethiopian and sends Philip to preach the Word of God to him.

Philip had preached the gospel to a big city congregation, but now he is called upon to preach the same gospel to just one man. He did not shy away from the task, but was just as comfortable in preaching to the one as to the many. History records other incidents in which ministers have had to preach to congregations of a similar size! On one occasion the American preacher Edward Payson travelled through a violent storm to get to church. Not long after entering the empty building the door opened again and another man entered for the service of worship. The man was a visitor and had come from a distance just to hear Dr Payson preach. That was enough for the preacher to abandon any thoughts of cancelling the service. Payson determined to speak, even if no one else came. It seemed that the severity of the storm had prevented everyone else from attending church that day. Some time later, during the following year, Edward Payson met the man again. 'I enjoyed the sermon', he told Dr Payson.

> I never heard a better one. Remember, I was sitting in the front, and whenever you said some things that were pretty hard, condemning men's sins, I'd glance around and see who you were getting at, and there was only me there! So I said to myself, 'He must mean you, Pompey, you old sinner!' Dr Payson, it was that sermon that set me thinking what a wicked man I've been, and since then I haven't missed a service at the church I attend.

The Lord honoured Edward Payson's faithfulness in preaching to that one man.

The Ethiopian was reading aloud from Isaiah 53, a gripping chapter of the Bible that is all about the sufferings of the promised Messiah. How extraordinary it is to find such a message in the very heart of the Old Testament! It is such a vivid portrait of the Lord Jesus Christ.

Imagine you were sorting through the contents of your attic and you discovered a few pictures painted by your great-great-great-grandfather. You look at them carefully. Some dusty old portraits of certain famous people of his generation – landowners and their families, lords and generals, but suddenly you lay your hand on another painting of his that really grabs your attention. In fact, this picture makes you step back in amazement; it is a perfect representation of your own daughter on the day of her wedding! The details of the gown and the expression of her face are utterly accurate. How astonishing! What an incredible experience, to set your eyes on that portrait!

This is how we should feel when we stumble across Isaiah 53 in the Old Testament Scriptures. The historical gap between the painting of this word-picture and the events it portrays only serves to heighten our sense of amazement. Isaiah lived many centuries before the coming and sufferings of Christ, and yet he wrote such an exact description of the death and burial of the Lord Jesus Christ. The words of Isaiah the eunuch had come to and was reading out loud were these:

> Like a sheep he was led to the slaughter and like a lamb before its shearers is silent, so he opens not his mouth. In his humiliation justice was denied him. Who can describe his generation? For his life is taken away from the earth (*Acts* 8:32–33).

What a wonderful text of Scripture with which to begin speaking about the Saviour!

5. PHILIP TOLD HIM THE GOOD NEWS ABOUT JESUS

'Then Philip opened his mouth, and beginning with this Scripture he told him the good news about Jesus' (*Acts* 8:35). This is a beautiful verse of Scripture. There is a simplicity here that we should admire and try to copy in our own personal evangelism.

David Jones of Llan-gan was a great preacher in the Welsh Calvinistic Methodist Church, and in one of his last letters he says, 'I am now endeavouring to reduce all my religion to one point, *"Christ is all"*.' This was Philip's message too! The Christ has come and his name is Jesus. 'Great indeed, we confess, is the mystery of godliness: He was manifested in the flesh' (*1 Tim.* 3:16). Oh, the drama of it all! Have you ever heard two women talking at the bus stop about the latest happenings in their favourite TV 'soap opera'? One woman asks the other if she saw the previous night's gripping episode. 'Wasn't it wonderful!' the other replies with excitement. 'I would not have missed it for the world!' But here is a true story that is more gripping by far!

The Lord Jesus is the eternal Son of God, the One by whom the Father made the heavens and the earth and everything in them. He is God, the Second Person of the blessed holy Trinity. He came into this world, entering his own creation and setting up his home among us. Mysteriously, he was born of a virgin mother, who held her little baby boy in her arms, and nursed him at her breast. Yes, the eternal Son of God took to himself a true body – one just like ours that needed air to breathe, food to eat, one that felt pain and grew tired and weary. He preached wonderful messages like, for example, the Sermon on the Mount, and he exercised great power over winds and waves, sickness and disease, the powers of darkness, and even death itself. All felt his authority because he was no ordinary man; he was the Lord Jesus, the very Son of God.

'He came to his own, and his own people did not receive him' (*John* 1:11). The majority of his own people

said, 'We will not have this man to reign over us', and
they refused his teaching and his claims. Only tax collec-
tors, prostitutes, fishermen, and anonymous ordinary folk
had anything to do with him. His enemies finally got their
hands on him. Leading figures in the Jewish nation lied
about him, falsely accused him, and intimidated the top
official in the Roman government into executing him as
a common criminal. 'Away with him! Crucify him!', they
cried. They all thought he was finished for ever when
they watched him die on the cross and saw him buried in
the tomb. 'Like a sheep he was led to the slaughter . . . for
his life is taken away.'

Do you know the true story of Jesus? To be truly com-
mitted to Jesus – to have what the Bible refers to as 'saving
faith' – you need to know who Jesus is and what he has
done to obtain salvation for sinners. However, this faith
is not just a matter of merely giving our intellectual
assent to a set of basic Bible facts about Jesus. It is much
more than that, but it is also never less than that. True,
saving faith must include the belief that Jesus, the Son of
God, came to earth to die for those sinners whom the
Father had given him, and that by suffering the death
penalty due for their sins, obtained salvation and everlasting life for all who believe. This is the message we
must grasp and make our very own. Faith receives and
rests upon the Lord Jesus Christ alone for salvation as he
is freely offered to us in the gospel. When we receive Christ
in this way everything about us changes.

At Golgotha's cross we also see what man is capable of
inflicting upon another man, as if we needed any more
reminders of the base brutality of sinful human nature.
One would think that the events of the twentieth century

would be sufficient to destroy the theory of the inherent goodness of human nature! But if you want the true indicator of the wickedness of human nature and the depravity of mankind, look to Calvary. God entered the world he had made and man, his fallen creature, nailed him to a cross in spiteful rebellion.

Because of the Fall of Adam into sin, all human beings have been born with a sinful nature that is hostile to God. In Adam we attempted to knock God off his throne, and when the Son of God appeared among us we took him to Calvary and nailed him to a cross. Certain members of the human race have been guilty of some terrible 'crimes against humanity' and we shudder at the thought of political leaders who have been tried and convicted of genocide, fratricide, and crimes against humanity. We are relieved (if not glad) to see them brought to justice to answer the serious charges brought against them. But what about our even more terrible sins against God? Shall we not face the justice of God for the charge of *deicide* for our part in the death of Jesus Christ? Only a great salvation and a great pardon can deliver us from such a sin as that!

But God was also doing something in the death of Christ. We must remember that men live and move and have their being in God. God mapped out all the events of Jesus' life – this is why Isaiah could prophesy so accurately about the coming and death of Christ centuries earlier. The death of Jesus was not a horrible accident. Calvary does not demonstrate that events had spiralled out of control while the Almighty was wringing his hands and looking on in helpless horror. No, instead, 'In Christ God was reconciling the world to himself' at Calvary

(2 *Cor.* 5:19). God was imputing the guilt of sin to the righteous and sinless Lamb of God and finding total satisfaction in his propitiatory death. On the cross the Lord Jesus reached the climax of his life of obedience to his Father's will – he was 'obedient to the point of death, even death on a cross' (*Phil.* 2:8). This was the hour for which he had come into the world: 'For even the Son of Man came not to be served but to serve, and to give his life as a ransom for many' (*Mark* 10:45). He had come, not only to seek us, but to save us as well (*Luke* 19:10). There was only one way for him to accomplish our salvation. Salvation could only be accomplished by his sacrificial death.

> Himself He could not save,
>   He on the cross must die,
> Or mercy cannot come
>   To ruined sinners nigh.
> Yes, Christ, the Son of God, must bleed,
> That sinners might from sin be freed.

The justice of God required it, for without the shedding of blood there is no remission of sin.

> Himself He could not save,
>   For justice must be done;
> And sin's full weight must fall
>   Upon a sinless One;
> For nothing less can God accept
> In payment for the fearful debt.

The Christian gospel clearly teaches that what was the most terrible action on the part of sinful man was also the most glorious act of our holy God, who willingly

presented his own Son as the sin-bearer, whose voluntary
death is the means of our redemption (*Rom.* 3:21–31).

> Himself He could not save,
>   For He the Surety[1] stood
> For all who now rely
>   Upon His precious blood;
> He bore the penalty of guilt
> When on the cross His blood was spilt.

As the reward for his obedience, Jesus Christ has
received from his Father all authority in heaven and on
earth. God has made Jesus Lord and Christ, Judge and
Saviour. Therefore, the biggest and most critical issue
facing men and women is what the Lord God is going to
do with them. Remember Christ Jesus has absolute power
over us. Jesus the Messiah asked his Father that the
heathen be given to him as his inheritance, and to him
they have been given (*Psa.* 2:8-12). He will do with you
what is holy, lawful, and righteous. Though we have been
ruined by the Fall and our own sins, and face judgment,
thanks be to God that he has not finished with us yet.

Praise God that 'the Son of Man has authority on earth
to forgive sins' (*Matt.* 9:6). Our only hope is in his mercy.
He can forgive us, but only because he has paid the price
of sin and satisfied divine justice on account of it. When
we stand before the divine Judge our only plea must be 'I
am guilty as charged, but save me, O God, for Jesus' sake.'
There is no hope for me unless Jesus Christ takes all the
guilt of my sins away. Only Jesus who suffered the punishment due for sin can rescue a sinner from hell. There

---

[1] *Surety:* a safeguard, legal security against loss; here, one who
becomes bound for another, a sponsor.

is no other way that both God's justice and his love can be satisfied and a sinner like me be forgiven. Jesus Christ, to whom I entrust myself, saves me. Salvation is provided for everyone who will come to God through Jesus Christ. Through Jesus who was crucified, you, too, may be pardoned.

Philip 'preached unto him Jesus' says the King James Version. 'Unto him', remarks old Cynddylan Jones:

> He pressed the Saviour on his acceptance. There is reason to fear that much of modern preaching is not personal enough . . . We have been preaching long enough *before* our congregations and *at* them, it is high time we should now preach *to* them. Let the beams of the sun fall broadly on your outstretched hand, and you hardly notice it; concentrate them on one spot and they burn. And the gospel light shines fully and broadly on our congregations, but how few the conversions! We diffuse the light instead of focusing it. We should concentrate it on the conscience and then it would burn its way to the very quick of the soul. 'He preached unto him Jesus.'[2]

6. PHILIP BAPTIZED HIM

The words Philip preached were life and heaven to the Ethiopian. The chariot drew alongside some kind of oasis. 'See, here is water! What prevents me from being baptized?' he said (*Acts* 8:36). The eunuch gave orders for the chariot to stop, and they both went down into the water and Philip baptized him. The servants looked on as their master professed his faith in Christ through this strange ceremony. Those who had heard Peter at Pentecost were told to repent and be baptized (*Acts* 2:38).

[2] Cynddylan Jones, *Studies in the Acts of the Apostles*, p. 192

Those in Samaria who 'believed Philip as he preached good news about the kingdom of God and the name of Jesus Christ . . . were baptized, both men and women' (*Acts* 8:12). It was the Ethiopian who took the initiative here: 'What prevents me from being baptized?' he cried. Nothing could prevent him from being baptized – not his sin, not his Gentile origin, not his condition as a eunuch. He was a true citizen of the kingdom of God, included within the New Covenant, a member of the church of Christ. And so they both went down into the water and Philip baptized this Gentile eunuch in the name of the Father and of the Son and of the Holy Spirit. The New Covenant age has truly come.

Philip's work being done, the Spirit of God suddenly carried him away and 'the eunuch saw him no more, and went on his way rejoicing' (*Acts* 8:39).

He had much cause to rejoice. The chapter from Isaiah the Ethiopian had been reading went on to say:

> When his soul makes an offering for sin, he shall see his offspring; he shall prolong his days; the will of the LORD shall prosper in his hand (*Isa.* 53:10).

The eunuch would never see his own offspring, but by faith he was joined to the One whose offspring are as numerous as the sand on the seashore and as the stars in heaven for number. The Lord's family is now the eunuch's family and, through personally witnessing to his new-found Saviour, the eunuch will become a 'father in the faith' to many.

Yes, the Ethiopian 'went on his way rejoicing' (*Acts* 8:39). Just as the gospel of Jesus brought joy to a city of Samaritans, so it brought joy to the heart of this most singular African man. Now, in Christ he has something to sing and shout about.

Can you remember the joy you felt when you trusted in the Lord at first?

> O happy day, that fixed my choice
>   On Thee, my Saviour and my God!
> Well may this glowing heart rejoice,
>   And tell its raptures all abroad.
>   *Philip Doddridge*

'I thought I could have leaped from earth to heaven at one spring when I first saw my sins drowned in the Redeemer's blood', said C. H. Spurgeon. He also said, 'It is an unfortunate thing for the Christian to become melancholy. If there is any man in the world that has a right to have a bright, clear face and a flashing eye, it is the man whose sins are forgiven him, who is saved with God's salvation.'

Therefore, shame on our gloomy faces, despondent looks, and joyless lives! Spirit-filled Christians are joyful Christians for 'the fruit of the Spirit is . . . joy . . .' (*Gal.* 5:22). We must not think that doom and gloom is holier than joy and gladness, or that a lack of assurance is more spiritual than a happy confidence in God's promises. Did you know that Christians are commanded to be happy? The apostle Paul commanded the Christians at Philippi to 'Rejoice in the Lord always' (*Phil.* 4:4). And he had good reason for giving such a command to them. A happy Christian is good for God, because he is honoured among men when his people are glad. Being happy is also good for ourselves, because it makes us strong: 'The joy of the LORD is your strength' (*Neh.* 8:10). Happy Christians are also good for the ungodly, because when they see Christians glad they long to be believers themselves. And when we are happy we bring comfort and cheer to our fellow Christians. 'Blessed are the people whose God is the LORD!' (*Psa.* 144:15).

> Come we that love the Lord,
> And let our joys be known;
> Join in a song with sweet accord,
> And thus surround the throne.
>
> The sorrows of the mind
> Be banished from the place;
> Religion never was designed
> To make our pleasures less.
>
> Let those refuse to sing
> That never knew our God;
> But children of the heavenly King
> May speak their joys abroad.
>
> The hill of Zion yields
> A thousand sacred sweets
> Before we reach the heavenly fields,
> Or walk the golden streets.
>
> There shall we see his face,
> And never, never, sin;
> There from the rivers of his grace
> Drink endless pleasures in.
>
> Then let our songs abound,
> And every tear be dry;
> We're marching through Immanuel's ground
> To fairer worlds on high.
>
> *Isaac Watts*